Ladner Crk.
March /14

"The Morning After"

Engineering camp, Coquihalla Pass, 1914

Steel Rails & Iron Men

Steel Rails & Iron Men

A PICTORIAL HISTORY OF THE KETTLE VALLEY RAILWAY

BARRIE SANFORD

whitecap

Copyright © 1990 by Barrie Sanford
Whitecap Books

First paperback edition, 2003

The information in this book is true and complete to the best of our knowledge.
All recommendations are made without guarantee on the part of the author or
Whitecap Books Ltd. The author and publisher disclaim any liability in connec-
tion with the use of this information. For additional information please contact
Whitecap Books Ltd., 351 Lynn Avenue, North Vancouver, British Columbia,
Canada, V7J 2C4.

Edited by Brian Scrivener
Front cover photograph from Penticton Museum 37–783; 1810A
Back cover photograph from the collection of Barrie Sanford
Cover design by Roberta Batchelor
Interior design by Carolyn Deby
Typography by CompuType, Vancouver, BC

Printed and bound in Canada by Friesens

National Library of Canada Cataloguing in Publication Data

Sanford, Barrie
    Steel rails and iron men: a pictorial history of the Kettle Valley Railway/
Barrie Sanford.

    Includes index.
    ISBN 1-55285-452-2

    1. Kettle Valley Railway—History—Pictorial works.   2. Railroads—British
Columbia—Okanagan–Similkameen—History—Pictorial works.   I. Title.

HE2810.K48S355 2003   385'.09711'62   C2002–911410–1

The publisher acknowledges the asssistance of the Canada Council and the
Cultural Services Branch of the Government of British Columbia in making this
publication possible. We acknowledge the financial support of the Government
of Canada through the Book Publishing Industry Development Program for our
publishing activities.

Coquihalla Canyon

Tunnel Excavation, Quintette Tunnels, Othello

CONTENTS

Introduction 1

Special Note to Railway Historians 3

Chapter 1. The Silver Dream 5

Chapter 2. The Kettle River Valley Railway 15

Chapter 3. The Nicola Branch 25

Chapter 4. McCulloch's Wonder 33

Chapter 5. Rough Quarries 61

Chapter 6. The Independent Years 75

Chapter 7. Hard Times 93

Chapter 8. The Second Mainline 107

Chapter 9. And Gone So Soon 121

Chapter 10. Remnant Railroad 129

Chapter 11. The Final Days 151

Chapter 12. Epilogue 161

Acknowledgements 162

Notes 162

Index 163

Tunnel Excavation, Quintette Tunnels, Othello

NTRODUCTION

I WAS BORN AND RAISED IN WHITE ROCK, WHICH WAS ONCE A QUIET SEASIDE COMMUNITY SOUTHEAST OF Vancouver before the metropolis grew up and engulfed it. White Rock was characterized by steep hills, sandy beaches and a railway line — the Great Northern Railway — which ran along the waterfront. It was from my early childhood exposure to that railway that I succumbed to the inexplicable magnetism generated by steel wheel moving on steel rail.

A mild climate and inexpensive housing made White Rock an attractive place for people to retire, and among the retirees seemed to be many former railroaders. I suppose a few railroaders had retired there some years before and wrote their friends to join them. For me it was a decided bonus. When I wasn't watching trains I could listen to old railroaders talk about trains. From them I learned about the Canadian Pacific, the Canadian National, the Pacific Great Eastern. I even learned about the faraway Toronto, Hamilton & Buffalo, and the barely pronounceable Timiskaming & Northern Ontario. But most of all I learned about a mystical railway line called "The KV."

On "The KV" the snowslides were the biggest, the grades the toughest, the runs the hardest. And locomotive firebox grates were the most unforgiving of the limitations of human muscle and human endurance. "The KV," it seemed, could only be described in superlatives.

Years later, in the fall of 1963, I noticed in an obscure section of a Vancouver paper an article stating that the Canadian Pacific Railway had been granted authority to discontinue passenger train service over the former Kettle Valley Railway. "The KV," it said, was nearly finished. Sensing a need for urgency, I travelled eastward to the interior of British Columbia to take what I thought would be my first and final look at the legendary railway about which I had heard so much. The line down the Tulameen Valley was magical. The Jura Loops fascinated me. But as the train burst forth from the forest above West Summerland and the great jewel of Okanagan Lake suddenly lay glittering several hundred feet below, with the tracks of "The KV" layered in three giant tiers on the faroff mountainside across the lake, I was flushed with amazement. Even superlatives seemed inadequate to describe this railway.

That train ride in 1963 sparked in me an intense curiosity. Visits to libraries in the search for information about the history of the Kettle Valley Railway proved fruitless. Although copious volumes were available about railways in the United States, and even the Canadian Pacific Railway was reasonably well documented, the Kettle Valley Railway rated no more than a passing reference. I set upon myself the task of documenting the Kettle Valley Railway story. The result was my book *McCulloch's Wonder*, which was published in 1977.

The title which I chose for the book was not of my own imagination. Rather it was a title which had been bestowed upon the railway by the engineering staff who built the line in tribute to the line's highly talented chief engineer, Andrew McCulloch. The book proved very popular, although those familiar with the railway's history know that I had to add nothing to make the Kettle Valley Railway story one of intense fascination.

That fascination has not ended. In 1980 the Kettle Valley Railway was much in the news as attempts were made to save the KVR tracks in spectacular Myra Canyon for tourist railway operations. The opening of the Coquihalla Highway in 1986 also brought a surge of interest in the rail line whose roadbed hung daringly to the cliff edges of the canyon followed by the new highway. In 1987 a new provincial park in the Quintette Tunnels at Othello inspires awe at this natural and man-made marvel. And the intriguing Shakespearian names along the Coquihalla Highway continue to be the source of questions asked by tourists driving this route.

The year 1989 witnessed the cessation of train operation on the final segment of trackage on the Kettle Valley Railway. In 1990 — the 75th anniversary of the Kettle Valley Railway's official opening in 1915 — authority was granted to tear up the rails. "The KV" has thus died.

But like an elderly man who passes after a long and useful life, the death of a railway should be viewed in the context of the life which was lived. The Kettle Valley Railway had a vibrant and exciting existence. It influenced the development of southern British Columbia in a myriad obvious and subtle ways. For this reason I concluded that the ending of "The KV" should not go without recognition. I offer this album in celebration of a great railway.

Barrie Sanford
1990

Postscript to 1990

Since 1990, when Steel Rails and Iron Men *first appeared in a hardcover edition, interest in the Kettle Valley Railway has continued to grow. While most of the tracks on the railway were removed in 1992, a short section of trackage at Summerland was left intact and returned to service as an operating railway – using a vintage steam locomotive – in 1995. The Kettle Valley Steam Railway carries more than 20,000 passengers a year, testimony to the enduring magnetism of the railway built by Andrew McCulloch and the thousands of labourers he commanded.*

The hardcover edition of Steel Rails and Iron Men *quickly sold out its initial printing. In the intervening years I have frequently been asked if a softcover edition could be produced to address the seemingly insatiable appetite of people wanting information about the Kettle Valley Railway. I am pleased to report that late in 2002 Whitecap Books made a commitment to reissue* Steel Rails and Iron Men *in a softcover edition.*

It seems particularly fitting that this reissue should be coming forth in the early years of the Twenty-first Century, just as the Kettle Valley Railway came forth into the world in the early years of the Twentieth Century. During the next decade or so the centenary of many important dates in the railway's history will be reached. There will be many occasions for us to pause and give recognition to the great legacy bestowed upon us by the pioneers of "The KV."

Barrie Sanford
2003

SPECIAL NOTE TO RAILWAY HISTORIANS

The Kettle Valley Railway was not static. Features about the line changed over time, and considerable confusion can result in any serious study of the railway without taking into account this evolution. Railway historians are advised to note the following:

Mile Points

Mileposts on the railway changed a number of times. Between Spences Bridge and Nicola mileages were originally calculated from Nicola, later Spences Bridge. Between Merritt and Brodie mileages were initially calculated from Penticton, later Merritt, later Spences Bridge. After 1961 all track between Brodie and Spences Bridge was combined into the Princeton Subdivision and mileages were calculated from Penticton. On the Carmi Subdivision mileages were initially calculated from the west end of Midway yard, but after 1931 mileages were calculated from Midway station, 0.4 miles east of the original point. On the Princeton Subdivision mileages were originally calculated from the switch to the lakeshore spur at Penticton yard, but after the new Penticton station was opened in 1941 they were calculated from the station, which added 0.2 miles to all points on the subdivision. To complicate matters, between Princeton and Brookmere, Great Northern mileages were originally used, as this portion of the KVR system was owned by the GN until 1945. On the Coquihalla Subdivision mileages were initially calculated as a continuation of the Princeton Subdivision; after 1941 they were calculated from Brookmere. To minimize potential confusion to readers, all mileage points cited in this book have been based on the October 1962 timetable, except for the Coquihalla Subdivision and other lines abandoned by that time. This standardization ensures that mileages cited in this book correspond with the final mileposts in place on the railway and with mileages shown in Roger Burrows's book *Railway Milepost: British Columbia/Volume 2*, which is a popular — and recommended — reference for railfans exploring the railways of southern British Columbia. Those referring to original source documents may encounter variations in mileages from those cited in this book for the reasons given.

Engineering Structures

These also changed over time and there are variations between different documents. Line engineering data cited in this book is based on the Kettle Valley Division 1947 Engineering Data Book.

Place Names

Place names used in this book generally cite the current name to minimize confusion. For example, Brookmere was called Otter Summit during the railway construction, and will appear by that name in any original source documents of the time. It was not renamed Brookmere until just before the railway opened.

Conflicting Information

One of the frustrations of historical research is dealing with conflicting information. A date or other information in the text marked with an asterisk (*) is based on what I judge to be the best available information, but some uncertainty exists.

PAYNE BLUFF, K. & S. RY., NEAR SANDON, B. C.

R. H. TRUEMAN & CO., PHOTO., VANCOUVER, B. C.

he Silver Dream

ALEXANDER MACKENZIE, CANADA'S TRANSITORY PRIME
MINISTER BETWEEN JOHN A. MACDONALD'S MUCH MORE
renowned two terms of office, once described British Columbia as
"a land of superlative difficulties." His remark was in reference
to the construction requirements of the projected Canadian Pacific Railway, a project
which Mackenzie thought economically unfeasible, or at least decidedly premature
in the country's development. When a few scant years later on November 7, 1885 a
steel hammer pounded a steel spike into a rail at Craigellachie, Mackenzie and his
remark were relegated to the largely forgotten tomes of history. But the remark had
continued relevance to the Canadian Pacific Railway. Its subsidiary company — the
Kettle Valley Railway — discovered in southern British Columbia what Mackenzie had
meant by his phrase "superlative difficulties."

It could be said that the Kettle Valley Railway had its genesis in the 1881 CPR
decision selecting the route of the transcontinental mainline across western Canada.
Ten years of detailed study by competent engineers working for the Canadian government had recommended that the railway be routed northwest from Winnipeg, ultimately penetrating the formidable Rocky Mountains through Yellowhead Pass west
of Edmonton. The directors of the newly created Canadian Pacific Railway corporation discarded this advice. Instead they chose to build directly west from Winnipeg.
The rationale, they said, was to protect the Canadian northwest from potential incur-
sion by American railways reaching across the international boundary line to the south.

But having argued this rationale, the CPR directors then swung the railway sharply
northward from Medicine Hat and entered British Columbia at Kicking Horse Pass,
the most northerly point on the entire Canadian Pacific mainline. Only after reaching
the southern limits of the Fraser Canyon at Hope did the railway return to within
reasonable proximity of the border the CPR had promised to protect.

At first this discrepancy was of little consequence. However, early in 1887 news
broke of a fabulously rich silver discovery near what is now the Kootenay District community of Nelson. The location was close to the international boundary, and practically within hours the first American had crossed the border to stake his silver fortunes
in the Kootenays. A thousand more were on his heels. Aided by the natural geogra-
phy of the southern interior and the close proximity to the border of the newly

FIGURE 1-1 *The
discovery of silver
in southern British
Columbia's Kootenay
District in 1887
prompted a stampede of
miners and railway
builders into the
southern interior of the
province. The majority of
the newcomers were
Americans, aided by the
easy geographic access
provided by the
Columbia River and its
numerous tributaries,
principally the Kootenay
River and the Kettle
River. Political and
economic concerns about
the prominent American
presence in the southern
interior resulted in
construction of a
competing Canadian
railway — the Kettle
Valley Railway —
eastward from the coast.
One such American-
controlled rail line which
was sought to be
countered was the Kaslo
& Slocan Railway,
pictured here at Payne
Bluff above Kaslo. The
Kaslo & Slocan's eastern
terminus was at Kaslo, a
half-day boat journey
from the mainline of its
parent, the Great
Northern Railway, at
Bonners Ferry.*

completed Northern Pacific Railroad, it took only a few weeks for the horde of incoming Americans to secure control of the Kootenays as effectively — and almost as dramatically — as if they had invaded by military force. The Canadian Pacific Railway could offer no protection. Its transcontinental route was simply too removed, and too blocked by mountains, to be of more than token influence.

The incident was not the first experience of this kind for the young province. A quarter-century earlier gold discoveries in the southern interior had also brought large numbers of Americans across the border. At that time the colonial governor, James Douglas, had commissioned Edgar Dewdney to blaze a trail from Hope across the southern interior. But the trail really did little more than accentuate the extreme disparities created by the parallel alignment of mountain ranges in British Columbia. The northward and southward alignment of the river valleys made it easy for the Americans to enter and leave the interior, while the intervening mountains made a very effective barrier against efforts to administer the colony from the coastal capital. Riding over the trail shortly after its completion, Douglas remarked that his journey was "...without exaggeration, compared to the passage of the Alps."[1]

The new Canadian Pacific Railway was supposed to prevent a repetition of such a political embarrassment. But it had not. What quickly evolved was the demand for a second railway in the province — a railway built well south of the CPR mainline which could effectively challenge the American domination of the southern interior and bring the wealth of the Kootenays to British Columbia's seaports. A forgotten sage coined a name for it: the Coast-to-Kootenay railway. The drive to build it would involve the Canadian Pacific Railway, the federal government, the provincial government and numerous other participants, sometimes co-operatively, sometime in bitter rivalry. Ultimately it would be the Kettle Valley Railway which would complete the task. A quarter-century of struggle would be required. But in the silver of the Kootenay mines all had found a dream.

The first serious proposal to build the Coast-to-Kootenay railway came from the American Daniel Corbin. In early 1888 Corbin chartered the Spokane Falls & Northern Railway in Washington State with the ambition of building northward to the Kootenays from Spokane. At the border Corbin found Canadian authorities reluctant to grant him a railway charter to reach Nelson out of fear that such a railway would merely strengthen American presence in the Kootenays. Corbin offered a railway between the coast and the Kootenays if Canadian authorities would allow him to build to Nelson. Perhaps it was only a ruse. In any case Corbin never built the Coast-to-Kootenay railway. After his railway to Nelson — the Nelson & Fort Sheppard Railway — was completed Corbin was content to use it to haul the Kootenay silver south.

The CPR attempted to counter Corbin's influence in the Kootenays by building its own rail line — the Columbia & Kootenay Railway — along the 25-mile unnavigable section of the Kootenay River between Robson and Nelson. From Robson steam vessels could operate, during season, up the Arrow Lakes and Columbia River to the CPR mainline at Revelstoke. By early 1891 the railway was complete and in operation. However, the Columbia & Kootenay Railway, like the earlier Dewdney Trail, was more symbolic than strategic. With the long water haul upstream to Revelstoke regularly disrupted by ice in winter and low water in summer, the C&K was ineffective in countering Corbin and the other Americans.

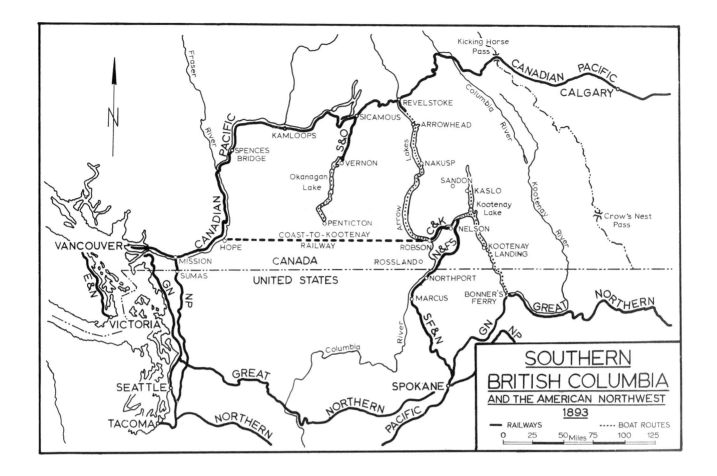

CPR President William Van Horne concluded that only a CPR through line across southern British Columbia to the coast would effectively secure the Kootenays into Canadian — and Canadian Pacific — control. As evidence of this conviction Van Horne assigned engineer J.A. Coryell to survey a railway route west from the C&K at Robson to the CPR mainline at Hope, 90 miles east of Vancouver.

Van Horne's action, though most immediately directed against Corbin, was really directed against James Jerome Hill. Throughout the early 1890s Hill built his Great Northern Railway across the American northwest, and its location was even closer to the boundary line than the earlier Northern Pacific. Moreover, previous experience had made Van Horne aware of Hill's disposition and talents. Hill had been one of the original directors of the CPR. In fact, he had been the one who invited Van Horne to join the management team. When they later quarreled, and the majority of the CPR directors supported Van Horne, Hill angrily left the CPR. He swore revenge, saying: "I'll get even with him if I have to go to hell for it and shovel coal!"[2]

That obsession did much to shape railway development in southern British Columbia. Hill built a number of rail lines which can be said served little function other than to make the CPR managers feel compelled to spend even more money in a foolish effort to counter him. Nor was corporate rivalry confined to the traffic departments and the ledger books. At Sandon in 1895 Hill's crews boldly destroyed a new CPR station and freight shed when the CPR built a competing rail line into that Slocan Valley community. It was the first of many direct confrontations between the two corporate rivals.

To protect southern British Columbia from the advances of the nearby Great Northern, Van Horne believed it necessary for the CPR to commence immediately building a rail line across the southern interior. Sharing that view was Thomas Shaughnessy, who was soon to succeed Van Horne as CPR president. However, Coryell's survey had revealed that the suggested Coast-to-Kootenay railway would be exceedingly expensive to construct. A more viable initial endeavour, the pair concluded, would be to link the Kootenays with the mainline east of Crowsnest Pass.

In 1897 work began. The last spike was driven at the south end of Kootenay Lake on October 15, 1898, a remarkably short time for a mountain railway nearly 300 miles in length. Simultaneously the CPR committed construction of its subsidiary Columbia & Western Railway westward from the west shore of the Columbia River across from the end of the C&K at Robson to the Boundary District, where major copper finds had been made shortly after the stampede to Nelson. By early 1900 CPR rails stretched westward to Midway, the midpoint of southern British Columbia.

Despite these obvious advances the CPR position in southern British Columbia was far from secure. To contain expenses the CPR had terminated the Crowsnest line at Kootenay Landing, at the south end of Kootenay Lake, and elected to cover the 50 miles to Nelson by lakeboats and rail barges until sufficient capital became available to complete the line. The CPR also passed on the immediate construction of a bridge across the Columbia River at Robson. Thus its line across southern British Columbia was really three disconnected segments of track relying on boats to link them. The mines of Nelson, Rossland and the Boundary still had no direct rail access to the rest of Canada. Direct rail connections were available only to the United States.

These direct rail connections were now exclusively in the hands of Jim Hill. As the CPR drove westward through Crowsnest Pass Hill bought out Corbin's line in the Kootenays. Then in March 1901 it was announced that Hill had secured control of the charter of the Vancouver, Victoria & Eastern Railway & Navigation Company. This company — which throughout history was known almost exclusively by its initials VV&E — had been formed by Vancouver and Victoria businessmen in 1897 with the objective of building the desired Coast-to-Kootenay Railway. Hill found in their failed enterprise a convenient vessel for his Canadian ambitions. In July 1901 Hill started construction of a rail line from Marcus up the Kettle River for the Boundary District, using the VV&E charter north of the border. Simultaneously another rail line was started into Crowsnest Pass. Work on both lines was undertaken with great vigour, an action which prompted the conservative Victoria *Colonist* to term the GN move "an invasion."[3]

The concern of the *Colonist*, shared by many British Columbians, was that Hill was using the VV&E charter only to build inexpensive feeder lines from the GN mainline to the rich mines of southern British Columbia, and that he would not build the much more costly Coast-to-Kootenay railway authorized by the VV&E's original charter. But others thought that an expanded GN network in the southern interior was the only assured way of getting the Coast-to-Kootenay railway built. If Hill did not build the line himself, the CPR would feel compelled to complete it to protect its existing investment in the interior. Strong lobby groups demanded that the government offer the VV&E substantial government aid to complete its authorized railway.

These demands posed problems for James Dunsmuir, the Vancouver Island coal baron who in June 1900 had became premier of British Columbia. Dunsmuir held a lucrative contract for supplying the CPR with coal for its locomotives. Championing aid to Hill was not the way to please a major customer. Moreover, any money allocated to the Coast-to-Kootenay railway would reduce the government money available to support another proposed rail undertaking — a railway from Edmonton across Seymour Narrows and down Vancouver Island to a connection with the Esquimalt & Nanaimo Railway, which by amazing coincidence Dunsmuir happened to own. Politically Dunsmuir could not be seen as opposing the much wanted Coast-to-Kootenay railway. But it would certainly offer some potential benefit if the public stopped clamouring to have it built.

Dunsmuir hit upon a novel idea. He would commission a government survey of the Hope Mountains — as documents of the day referred to the Cascade Range — which was the most difficult section of the route between the coast and Midway. Dunsmuir said that such a survey would give the government accurate data to use in its dealings with Hill and the CPR. In July 1901 Dunsmuir commissioned Edgar Dewdney, the man who forty years earlier had constructed the Dewdney Trail, to take charge of the government survey. The survey was conducted that summer and fall.

Dewdney's report was anything but encouraging to those seeking early construction of the Coast-to-Kootenay railway. Dewdney established three possible routes for a railway between Hope and Princeton, one via Allison Pass, one via Coquihalla Pass and one via a new pass the expedition named Railroad Pass. However, Dewdney emphasized that all three routes involved very heavy construction and long stretches of severely adverse gradients. He added:

> The result of the survey shows that the Hope Mountains cannot be crossed without encountering serious engineering difficulties which necessitate a very large expenditure of money, and I know of nothing so pressing, either in the way of development or along any line which might be determined on to warrant its construction.[4]

From an engineering viewpoint the survey was well done. And Dewdney accurately forecast that Allison Pass would give much less problem with snow than Coquihalla Pass. But it is obvious that Dunsmuir controlled the political agenda. Dunsmuir had instructed Dewdney to examine potential railway routes only between Hope and Princeton, a directive which dictated the outcome of the report even before the survey began. A railway between Hope and Princeton would be very expensive, with little prospect of being economically feasible on the basis of local traffic. Only as part of a through route to the rich traffic areas of the Boundary and Kootenays could a railway across the Hope Mountains possibly make economic sense.

Dewdney never commented on this fundamental shortcoming in his report, obediently maintaining strict public silence on his personal thoughts about the survey until Dunsmuir was no longer premier. In later years Dewdney expressed the viewpoint that a railway to the Kootenays was quite feasible if a routing was chosen using the CPR mainline to Spences Bridge, then following the Nicola and Similkameen River systems eastward. Dewdney noted that such a line — going around rather than across the Hope Mountains — would be about 100 miles longer than any of the routes suggested in his report, but would be much less expensive to construct and of decidedly better grades, factors which could potentially more than offset the additional hauling distance.

△ FIGURE 1-2 *Three handsome CPR inland lake vessels docked at Arrowhead, at the north end of Upper Arrow Lake. The tracks in the foreground lead from the CPR mainline at Revelstoke, 27 miles to the north. The boats and branch lines provided a tenuous link between the CPR and the Kootenay mines. Low water in summer or ice in winter easily disrupted service on the inland waterways. As the Kootenays grew, so did the demand for direct rail connections with the coast.*
CITY OF VANCOUVER
ARCHIVES (CVA 2/38)

Dewdney never presented this more viable alternative to Dunsmuir or to the public in his report. Perhaps Dewdney only came to this viewpoint later. In any case the damage had been done. The report Dunsmuir directed helped forestall the Coast-to-Kootenay railway another eight years. Hill and the CPR would slash at each other in the Kootenay Lake country, in the Crowsnest and in the Boundary District for nearly another decade before turning their attention to crossing the Hope Mountains for the coast.

FIGURE 1-3

◁ FIGURE 1-3 *In 1898 the CPR commenced construction of the Columbia & Western Railway westward from Robson over the Monashee Mountains to the Boundary District. This picture shows a C&W survey crew at work near Christina Lake in 1899. Members of the party (left to right): B.W. Lamont, W.A. Patterson, D.A. Finlayson and Andrew McCulloch, assistant engineer. McCulloch was involved with the engineering of most of the CPR-controlled railway lines in southern British Columbia, and went on to become chief engineer of the Kettle Valley Railway.* COURTESY ANDREW McCULLOCH FOUNDATION

FIGURE 1-4

△ FIGURE 1-4 *Summerland, on the west shore of Okanagan Lake, showing the CPR vessel "Okanagan" at the dock, and a railcar awaiting loading from the fruit warehouse alongside. The railcar will be taken by barge to Okanagan Landing, thence over the Shuswap & Okanagan Railway to the CPR mainline at Sicamous. The Kettle Valley Railway entered the Okanagan Valley from the west by following the benchlands in the distance down to Penticton, out of the picture to the left.* COLLECTION OF BARRIE SANFORD

FIGURE 1-5

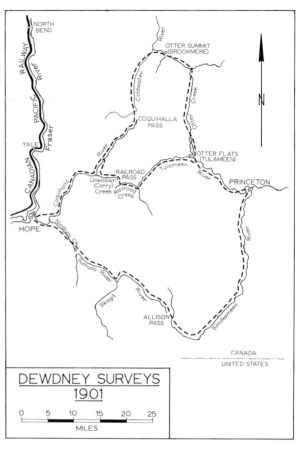

◁ FIGURE 1-5 *Coquihalla Pass, as it appeared to members of the Dewdney Expedition in 1901 prior to the construction of the Kettle Valley Railway. The view is looking southwest, down the river canyon, from a point which would later be about Mile 19.8 on the Coquihalla Subdivision of the Kettle Valley Railway. In order to maintain allowable gradient, the railway had to cut across the face of these canyon walls.* COLLECTION OF BARRIE SANFORD

FIGURE 1-6

△ FIGURE 1-6 *Coquihalla Pass, as seen looking southwest from the 6630-foot-high vantage point of Mount Thynne, south of Brookmere, showing the strategic gap through which the Kettle Valley Railway pierced the Hope Mountains. Vantage points such as this were used by the early railway surveyors to gain appreciation of overall topography, a task vital in the age before helicopters, aerial photography and satellite mapping.*

The treeless mountain on the left is Mount Coquihalla. The snowcapped peak beyond it is Mount Baker, rarely seen from the rugged interior except by airplane. The sharp peak to the right of centre is Iago Needle, so named for its location back of the site of former Iago station on the Kettle Valley Railway. Below it and slightly to the left is the Coquihalla Highway near its summit point. PHOTO BY BARRIE SANFORD

FIGURE 1-7

▷ FIGURE 1-7 *The life of the early railway engineer was not easy. Survey work continued year round, often under conditions of severe winter weather. These tents were ''home'' to a C&W survey party near Cascade in the winter of 1899-1900.* COURTESY ANDREW McCULLOCH FOUNDATION

△ FIGURE 2-1 *Entry into foreign territory was not restricted to American railroads. In 1901 - 1902 the Canadian-owned Kettle River Valley Railway and its affiliate Republic & Kettle River Railway constructed a rail line from Grand Forks southward to the Washington State mining community of Republic. This modest trackage marked the beginning of the Kettle Valley Railway which later expanded westward across the Hope Mountains to connect with coastal British Columbia. Here locomotive No. 1 assists in laying track near Curlew, Washington, in early 1902. This Baldwin-built 4-4-0 was acquired secondhand by the railway in October 1901 and inherited the nickname "The Tin Whistle". The railway owned two other locomotives, both 4-6-0's, delivered in February 1902.* COLLECTION OF DAVE WILKIE

he Kettle River Valley Railway

THE KOOTENAYS HAD BEEN THE BATTLEGROUND BE-
TWEEN CANADIAN AND AMERICAN RAILWAY INTERESTS
in the 1890s. After the turn of the century the battleground widened
to encompass the Boundary District and Kettle River country to
the west. Canadian Pacific was the first to strike a claim on this new territory, when
it completed its Columbia & Western Railway to Grand Forks in September 1899. Soon
it had extended westward to Midway and to the mountaintop copper camp of Phoenix, centre of the Boundary District's vast endowment of copper ore. Hill followed
with his Great Northern. But between the two giants a small independent railway
took seed and germinated. This was a rail line born in the valley of the Kettle River
— the Kettle Valley Railway.

The Kettle Valley Railway was the brainchild of Tracy Holland. Holland had come
west from Ontario to supervise the affairs of the Grand Forks Townsite Company. His
enterprising mind quickly recognized business potential in the American community
of Republic, 35 miles to the south of Grand Forks. Republic had copper ore in abun-
dance. But it was without rail connections, a deficiency Holland saw only as opportu-
nity. With the Phoenix mines already pouring out more ore than the CPR could carry,
Holland had no difficulty envisioning a railway of his own soon overflowing with
Republic ore destined for the smelter at Grand Forks.

Holland communicated his idea to several associates in the Dominion Permanent Loan Company and the Trusts & Guarantee Company, which agreed to jointly
finance the proposed railway along the Kettle River and Curlew Creek to Republic.
A charter was secured from the State of Washington for the American portion of the
route. This was legally titled the Republic & Kettle River Railway, although the name
was later changed to the more ambitious title Spokane & British Columbia Railway.

A charter was also sought from Ottawa for the Kettle River Valley Railway, with
authority to build a line of railway over the three miles distance from Grand Forks
to the international boundary at Carson and for several branch lines, principally a
50-mile-long line from Grand Forks up the North Fork of the Kettle River to Franklin
Camp. On May 23, 1901 the charter act of the Kettle River Valley Railway was officially assented to by the Government of Canada, thus formally opening the pages of history on one of Canada's most colourful railways.

▷ FIGURE 2-2
Decorated with Stars and Stripes and Union Jacks, the first official passenger train over the KRVR-R&KR heads south from Grand Forks on April 12, 1902. The 300 passengers on board are destined for Republic. But not the train. Tracy Holland had declared the railway complete, notwithstanding the absence of the last five miles of track, and the passengers that day would spend more time travelling by wagon than railway coach.
COLLECTION OF
BARRIE SANFORD

FIGURE 2-2

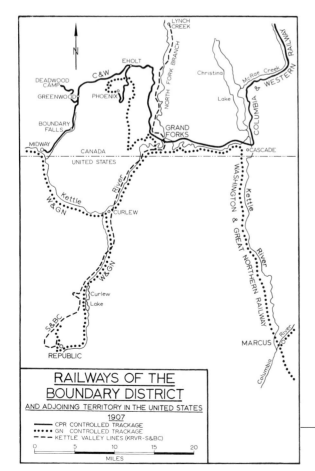

RAILWAYS OF THE
BOUNDARY DISTRICT
AND ADJOINING TERRITORY IN THE UNITED STATES
1907
—— CPR CONTROLLED TRACKAGE
•••• GN CONTROLLED TRACKAGE
‒‒‒ KETTLE VALLEY LINES (KRVR-S&BC)

0   5   10   15   20
MILES

Although Holland returned from Ottawa with his needed charter, the people of Grand Forks were annoyed by the year delay since he had first proposed his railway to Republic. As a consequence Holland's railway was dubbed the ''Hot Air Line,'' a title which stuck with his corporation for the rest of its days. Undaunted, Holland awarded a contract for the line's construction on August 31, 1901. Work began immediately.

As well as earning the railway a dubious nickname, the delay at Ottawa had proved costly to Holland in another way. During 1901 Jim Hill had started construction of a railway up the Kettle River from Marcus. With Hill promising to extend the line south to Republic, Holland's easy moneymaking railway scheme had suddenly turned into a life or death battle with Hill's giant railroad empire. Holland promptly persuaded local land owners to refuse Hill right-of-way land for his VV&E. A court injunction was also secured blocking the VV&E from crossing the KRVR, which it would have to do to enter Grand Forks.

Retaliation was swift in coming. Early on the morning of January 5, 1902 a force of men from Hill's subsidiary Washington & Great Northern Railway, which was building the parallel line to Republic, raided the R&KR right-of-way near Curlew and began pulling down a trestle built by the smaller company. A Sunday morning was chosen for the raid, no doubt in the expectation that few R&KR men would be on the site. But the few R&KR men at the trestle promptly secured reinforcements and the W&GN attackers were repelled. The newcomer had made it clear that it too could play the game by Hill's rules.

The tenacity of the "Hot Air Line," along with the injunctions and other delaying tactics, allowed the KRVR-R&KR to sprint ahead in tracklaying, and as of April 12, 1902 Holland formally declared his railway complete. That day both Grand Forks and Republic were gaily decorated in Union Jacks and Stars and Stripes, and a special train ran over the line from Grand Forks to introduce local people to their new railway. Tracy Holland personally drove a gold spike into the track at Republic. Enthusiasm was such that nearly everyone was willing to overlook Holland's eagerness in calling the railway complete. The "last" spike was actually driven into a single pair of rails in the centre of Republic, five miles from the nearest piece of trackage on the remainder of the railway!

Holland's railway was physically finished not long afterwards, but Holland was hardly comfortable. Hill was soon into Republic, and Grand Forks as well. The KRVR thought it had Hill successfully fenced out of Grand Forks as a result of its injunction prohibiting the VV&E from crossing the KRVR. But when the citizens of Grand Forks

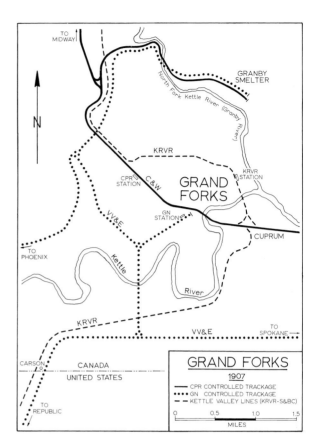

woke up on November 10, 1902 they discovered that they had a new railway; Hill's crews had installed a diamond crossing over the KRVR and laid track into the city during the night. Immediately after discovering the offense the KRVR positioned one of its locomotives in the middle of the diamond crossing, thus blocking any further inroads by the VV&E. When VV&E crews arrived in large number violence seemed imminent, but later in the day the KRVR removed the locomotive after Hill threatened other retaliation.

Competition from the Great Northern made the new railway's existence perilous from the outset. Moreover, the Republic ores proved difficult to smelt using conventional smelting processes, and this reduced what traffic there was to split between the two competing railways. Finding the stress too great, Tracy Holland resigned in 1902 without an immediate replacement of similar calibre to take over the railway's management.

The new management formed a separate corporation — Kettle Valley Lines — to act as a holding company for vesture of the Canadian and American charters. It also turned its attention to the earlier dream of a railway north to Franklin Camp. The resurrected project was expanded to reach beyond Franklin Camp through Vernon to the Nicola Valley, where extensive coal fields promised a good potential traffic destined to the smelters of the Boundary District. After a false start in 1905 work began on June 16, 1906 grading the roadbed for the projected rail line through the city centre of Grand Forks. Work advanced at a steady pace, but the rate of progress was hardly

△ FIGURE 2-3 *The financial viability of the Kettle River Valley Railway was immediately*
threatened by the Great Northern Railway and its several affiliated companies, which also
built a rail line to Republic during 1902. In retaliation the KRVR attempted to legally block the
Great Northern's VV&E from crossing the KRVR to enter Grand Forks. However, on the morning
of November 10, 1902 the citizens of Grand Forks awoke to discover that the VV&E had
constructed a level crossing across the KRVR during the night. The KRVR responded by
positioning one of its locomotives across the diamond to prevent the VV&E from laying any
further track. This picture shows the tense scene as it existed that morning. PROVINCIAL ARCHIVES
OF BRITISH COLUMBIA (NEG 44204)

impressive. Not until over a year later did the first train run over the line through
Grand Forks, and when work on the extension ceased entirely track had been laid
only to Lynch Creek, 18 miles north of Grand Forks. Later it would be extended about
two miles to reach the Rock Candy fluorite mine. But even this brought the line less
than halfway to the first destination of Franklin Camp and a long way from the
promised goal of the Nicola Valley. Curiously, the line did reach the Nicola Valley
some years later by a different route and under quite different circumstances.

That expansion took place under the auspices of the CPR, which in 1910, secured
effective control of the company and used the charter to build westward from Midway
to the coast as the final link in its line across southern British Columbia. Under CPR
control the company dropped the awkward ''River'' from its original corporate title
and became simply the Kettle Valley Railway. This was a formal acknowledgement
of the title by which the line had commonly been known all along. Over time the
name came to be applied to the entire trackage across southern British Columbia,
even on into Alberta. Such was the magic of the Kettle Valley Railway. But legally
speaking, the company's holdings embraced only the line west of Midway and the
limited trackage around Grand Forks.

Because of the close association between the CPR and KVR after 1910 the two
companies agreed in 1913 to share facilities in Grand Forks. KVR locomotives
commenced using a new roundhouse which the CPR built and CPR trains used a new
''union'' station which the KVR constructed in downtown Grand Forks. Access to this
station was considerably more convenient for the public than the CPR station, which

FIGURE 2-4

SPOKANE & BRITISH COLUMBIA

RAILWAY COMPANY

28   1911

PASS --A.McCulloch----------
Chief Engineer
Kettle River Valley Railway Co.
UNTIL DECEMBER 31st, 1911
UNLESS OTHERWISE ORDERED

COUNTERSIGNED:

O.E.Fisher   *N. J. Beck.*

PRESIDENT

◁ FIGURE 2-4
*Annual Pass for
1911 issued by the
Spokane & British
Columbia Railway to
Andrew McCulloch, then
chief engineer of the
Kettle Valley Railway.*
COURTESY ANDREW
McCULLOCH COLLECTION

▽ FIGURE 2-5 *Locomotive No. 2 switches ore cars up to the main line from the spur to
Eureka Gulch, west of Republic. The tracks on the left are those of the rival
Great Northern.* COLLECTION OF DAVE WILKIE

FIGURE 2-5

△ FIGURE 2-6 *This picture is believed to be one of the first trains over the North Fork line of the Kettle River Valley Railway at Lynch Creek, approved by the Railway Commission for operation on January 21, 1909.* COURTESY VINTAGE VISUALS (RRR003)

the company had built outside the City of Grand Forks as a result of a property dispute when it entered the Kettle Valley in 1899.

The geographic separation between the original trackage around Grand Forks and the much greater trackage to the west resulted in the expanded Kettle Valley Railway giving steadily diminished attention to the trackage of its birth. In its acquisition of the KVR the CPR deliberately avoided the doubtful American trackage held by Kettle Valley Lines, and the line to Republic was allowed to languish by the S&BC. The drop in copper prices after the First World War killed the last remaining copper trade, and in September 1919 service on the line ceased entirely.

After that date the North Fork line effectively became part of the CPR. Train service on the line was provided by a CPR locomotive, usually 3113, from Grand Forks. Starting in 1926 the line even appeared in CPR employee timetables rather than the timetables of the KVR which legally owned the line. The line was abandoned in 1935.

The construction achievements in the Kettle Valley by the Kettle Valley Railway and its numerous associated companies were hardly of strategic consequence in the saga of railroading in southern British Columbia. But the Kettle Valley had given name to a company which had a manifest destiny to fulfill in the province. The construction of the Kettle Valley Railway west from Midway across the Hope Mountains to the coast brought to fruition the Coast-to-Kootenay railway dream.

▽ FIGURE 2-7 *The CPR station at Grand Forks. When the CPR built its subsidiary*
Columbia & Western Railway through the Kettle Valley in 1899 it could not secure land
within the City of Grand Forks on terms it considered acceptable. Consequently the CPR built
this station about a mile and a half west of the city centre, outside the city limits, in an area
generally known as "West End." Starting in 1913 CPR passenger trains used the Kettle Valley
Railway station in the centre of the city. PROVINCIAL ARCHIVES OF BRITISH COLUMBIA
(CAT. HP43961; NEG. B9030).

FIGURE 2-7

△ FIGURE 2-8 *Grand Forks "union" station, built in downtown Grand Forks by the Kettle Valley Railway as part of its 1912 agreement with the CPR for sharing facilities. Prior to the station's opening in May 1913 Canadian Pacific passenger trains stopped at the CPR station outside the city limits, but after that date CPR trains diverted off the main track at either Cuprum or City Junction and into the city centre. The station was also used by KVR trains operating on the North Fork line and to Republic. In 1921 the bridge over the Kettle River between Cuprum and the downtown station was damaged by high water. Thereafter CPR routed passenger trains to and from the downtown station only via the trackage from City Junction at the west end of town. Eastbound trains headed into the station and westbound trains backed in. This awkward arrangement continued until 1952 when CPR trains reverted to using the original station.* PROVINCIAL ARCHIVES OF BRITISH COLUMBIA (CAT. HP44214; NEG. B9621)

Kettle Valley Railway Dateline

Grand Forks Operation

1901-05-23	Dominion government granted charter for the Kettle River Valley Railway.
1901-08-31	KRVR announced that contract for construction of line between Grand Forks and Republic awarded.
1901-10-28	First spike on Republic line driven.
1902-04-12	"Last" spike driven at Republic. Line declared open.
1902-11-10	KRVR placed locomotive across VV&E diamond in effort to block GN from entering Grand Forks.
1905-07-31	Construction of line up North Fork of Kettle River commenced. Work soon halted.
1906-06-16	Construction of line up North Fork of Kettle River resumed.
1907-06-24	First KRVR train operated through downtown Grand Forks.
1909-01-21	Railway Commission approved North Fork line between Grand Forks and Mile 19.0 for regular operation.
1911-04-04	Kettle River Valley Railway legally renamed Kettle Valley Railway.
1912-06-22	Announcement made that CPR and KVR would share station and facilities at Grand Forks.
1913-05-01	CPR trains commenced using downtown station at Grand Forks.
1919-09-27	Spokane & British Columbia Railway ceased operation.
1921-07-08	Announcement made that all assets of S&BC sold.
1935-09-27	Railway Commission approved abandonment of North Fork Subdivision.
1952-09-28	CPR passenger trains ceased using "union" depot in Grand Forks.

NORTHBOUND TRAINS INFERIOR DIRECTION			NORTH FORK SUBDIVISION		SOUTHBOUND TRAINS SUPERIOR DIRECTION		
SECOND CLASS					SECOND CLASS		
865	Miles from Carson	Telegraph Office		Telegraph Calls	866		
Mixed *l* Thurs.			STATIONS		Mixed *a* Thurs.		
	.0		CARSON				
	2.0		G. N. JUNCTION 2.0				
10.00	4.0	D	★ GRAND FORKS WR B O (City Stn.)		13.00		
	5.5		WESTEND CWR 1.5				
f 10.10	7.5		SMELTER LAKE 2.0		f 12.50		
f 10.20	10.5		★ CAESAR 3.0		f 12.40		
f 10.30	12.0		★ TROUTDALE 1.5		f 12.20		
f 10.38	15.0		★ HUMMING BIRD 3.0		f 12.10		
f 10.51	18.5		★ BANNOCK 3.5		f 11.56		
f 10.56	19.5		★ STANWELL 1.0		f 11.51		
f 11.10	22.2		LYNCH CREEK Y 2.7		f 11.40		
11.15	23.9		ARCHIBALD 1.7		11.35		
a Thurs. 865			★ No passing track		*l* Thurs. 866		

No. 866 will wait at Archibald until No. 865 arrives.
Maintenance of Way Employees will provide unattended flagging protection as per Rules 51 and 52—Maintenance of Way Rules and Instructions. Train and Enginemen affected will see that requirements of Rule 52-B are complied with.

◁ FIGURE 2-9 CPR *Timetable extract for the North Fork Subdivision in 1929. Even though the North Fork line was legally still part of the KVR, the fact that it appeared in a CPR timetable accurately reflects the almost complete divorce of the "new" Kettle Valley Railway west of Midway from the Grand Forks trackage of its birth.* COLLECTION OF BARRIE SANFORD

FIGURE 2-9

The Nicola Branch

THE SECOND RAIL LINE WHICH WAS TO BECOME PART OF
THE KETTLE VALLEY RAILWAY WAS BUILT IN THE NICOLA
Valley, 200 miles to the west of the Kettle Valley where the railway
had its birth. Like the region of the railway's genesis, the Nicola
Valley was generously endowed with mineral wealth, in this case coal. Deep deposits
of bituminous coal lay beneath the valley basin, and at numerous points the seams
were exposed in the valley cut by the Nicola River during its 50-mile journey northwest from Nicola Lake to the Thompson River at Spences Bridge.

The coal was well known to the early natives long before the white man's coming. It is known too that coal from the Nicola Valley made its way northward to the
blacksmith shops of the Cariboo during the Barkerville gold rush. However, it appears
that no official notice of the coal exposures was made until 1872 when members of
the Sandford Fleming survey expedition came upon them while seeking a route for
the proposed transcontinental railway. Fleming viewed the coal as an obvious point
in favour of the suggested railway route from Kamloops via Nicola Lake and Coquihalla Pass to Hope. But the lower grades of the Thompson and Fraser rivers route
resulted in the rejection of the Nicola Valley as the route for the CPR mainline. Loco-
tive coal, the CPR decided, would come from the Vancouver Island mines of the Dunsmuir family or the mines of Lethbridge.

Nevertheless, interest in a railway to the Nicola Valley was not lost. Early in 1891
a group of mainly Ontario businessmen petitioned the provincial government for a
charter for the Nicola, Kamloops & Similkameen Coal & Railway Company. Among
the petitioners were Sandford Fleming, the first to recognize the potential of the Nicola coal fields, and William Hamilton Merritt, the man for whom the chief community of the Nicola Valley would later be named. On April 20, 1891 the provincial
government granted the group their charter, along with that granted a rival group using the name Nicola Valley Railway.

Initially, neither group undertook any construction beyond a ceremonial sod turning by the Nicola Valley Railway. This changed abruptly one spring morning in 1905
when James Dunsmuir vengefully locked out his Vancouver Island coal miners after
they had the audacity to seek a pay raise of 25 cents per day, an action which threatened to leave every CPR locomotive firebox in the province stone cold for want of

FIGURE 3-1 *The
most prominent
feature of the CPR's
Nicola Branch — later
part of the Kettle Valley
Railway — was the
324-foot-long tunnel
under Ten Mile Hill,
later Mile 168.2 of the
Princeton Subdivision.
The tunnel was
distinguished by portals
made of cut stone,
quarried and placed by
hand using technology
only modestly changed
from that deployed in the
construction of the
Egyptian pyramids. The
tunnel is the only part
of the line which has
remained unchanged
since its construction in
1905-06.* PHOTO BY
BARRIE SANFORD

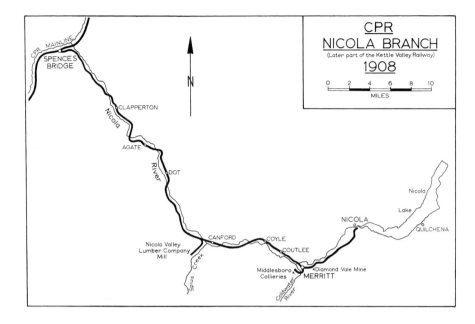

CPR
NICOLA BRANCH
(Later part of the Kettle Valley Railway)
1908

coal. The CPR hastily secured the charter of the Nicola, Kamloops & Similkameen Coal & Railway from its founders, and in June 1905 construction was commenced on a rail line from Spences Bridge to Nicola. Published government reports setting the probable coal reserves of the Nicola Valley at 175 million tons offered the CPR assurances that the new line would eliminate its dependence upon the Dunsmuir mines.

In announcing that it was committing construction of the line to the Nicola Valley, the CPR stated that the railway would later be extended through to the Boundary District, thus providing rail connections between the coast and the Kootenays. When questioned during a visit to Vancouver in September 1905, CPR President Thomas Shaughnessy affirmed the company's intention to build, saying: ''...preparations are being made for a gradual extension through the Similkameen Valley with the ultimate intention of reaching Midway.''[5] Shaughnessy emphasized that immediate attention would be given only to construction of the line as far as Nicola Lake.

The Nicola Branch, as the CPR formally named the line when it opened, was generally of easy construction. A few sections of heavy rock work and one tunnel were involved in the first 20 miles from Spences Bridge, and eight crossings of the Nicola River were employed. But the ruling grade on the line was only 0.6%, modest indeed for British Columbia's rugged terrain. The contract allowed $1.5 million for the 47 miles of line between Spences Bridge and Nicola.

Construction work was done almost exclusively by men and horses. Some 1500 men were employed, ironically many of them locked-out Vancouver Island coal miners who hoped to get back at Dunsmuir by helping build the railway designed to end his lucrative coastal coal monopoly. The pay rate for labourers was $2.25 per day. Although that was the standard pay rate of the day, the contractors reported shortages of manpower and materials. As well, the reopening of Dunsmuir's mines reduced the urgency to build the railway. Not until April 1907 did the Nicola Branch formally open. Three times per week mixed train service was initially offered, with supplementary freight train service as warranted. A two-stall enginehouse was built at Nicola for engines laying overnight at the end of the line.

The completion of the Nicola Branch spurred the coal industry of the Nicola Valley. The first operating mine of the Nicola Valley was the Nicola Valley Coal & Coke Company, which opened a mine on the hillside across the Coldwater River from Merritt under the name Middlesboro Collieries. In early January 1907 coal from the

△ FIGURE 3-2 *Although this photograph was taken in the 1980s, the pleasant scenery of the Nicola Valley has not changed greatly since the CPR Nicola Branch was constructed three-quarters of a century earlier. This view shows the rail crossing of the Nicola River at Mile 156.5 (Princeton Subdivision), just above Dot. The bridge pictured here was not part of the original construction. When the Nicola Branch was built in 1905-07 all the major bridges on the line were wooden Howe Truss spans. Wooden bridges normally had an effective life of about 15 to 20 years before the wood commenced to rot and had to be replaced. This particular bridge is 163 feet long and was built by the Canadian Bridge Company in 1923-24 as part of a general upgrading of the original line undertaken at that time.*

No high-quality photos of the Nicola Branch Howe Truss bridges appear to exist. As well as being of interest in themselves, the early Nicola Branch bridges had the distinction of being the first documented engineering work in British Columbia performed by a female engineer. Miss Lota Alice Foss was an engineering student at the University of Minnesota — the first female to enroll in engineering in that state — when she secured a job during the summer of 1905 checking bridge plans on the Nicola Branch. Little is known about Miss Foss's later engineering achievements, although it was recorded that she subsequently married another engineer she met on the Nicola Branch that summer. PHOTO BY BARRIE SANFORD

△ FIGURE 3-3 *The station at Dot. As typical of many small community stations, Dot station had a bay window which would allow the operator to view the tracks in either direction without leaving his desk. It also had a baggage room and upstairs living quarters for the operator. In 1941 the community of Dot gained national recognition by being the smallest polling division in the country, with five registered voters. Dot was named after Dalton "Dot" Marpole, son of CPR General Superintendent Richard Marpole, who owned a ranch nearby.* PHOTO BY BARRIE SANFORD

▷ FIGURE 3-4 *Timetable for the Nicola Branch dated June 2, 1907, two months after the line's official opening. Note that Merritt is shown only as a flagstop, unlike the obligatory stop at most other stations on the line. Although the developing coal mines of Merritt would quickly make it the premier community of the Nicola Valley, in 1907 it was a mere hamlet renamed from its earlier title of Forksdale.* COLLECTION OF BARRIE SANFORD

Middlesboro mine was tested in a CPR locomotive, and the locomotive crew pronounced the coal to be the best they had ever used. Consequently, as of January 22, 1907 when the first load of coal left the Nicola Valley, the CPR did its best to secure the mine's output for its coal chutes on the mainline as far east as Revelstoke and for its boats on Okanagan Lake. Diamond Vale Collieries, Pacific Coast Collieries and the Inland Coke & Coal Company also opened mines. By 1910 approximately 50 cars of coal per day were travelling down the Nicola Branch to Spences Bridge.

Quickly following the Merritt coal mines were sawmills. The demand for railway crossties and mine timbers provided an instant market for the output of the sawmills, and numerous mills sprang up along the railway. The largest of the mills was that of the Nicola Valley Lumber Company, which opened a mill on the south side of the railway just below Canford. Other mills were built at Merritt. The seasonal movement of cattle from the plateau ranches, most notably the famous Douglas Lake Cattle Company, supplemented the coal and lumber traffic.

The transportation of coal, lumber and cattle traffic often made the mixed train between Spences Bridge and Nicola both lengthy and slow. The citizens of the Nicola Valley constantly campaigned for separate freight and passenger train service, but except for a brief period of CPR benevolence during the later building of the Kettle Valley Railway when large amounts of construction material were being delivered, mixed train service was the only passenger service which was operated throughout most of the line's history.

Merritt also regularly complained about the CPR rate for hauling coal to the coast. The rate, which generally hovered around $1.80 per ton, was considered to be responsible for excluding Merritt coal from the domestic coal market at the coast. Despite complaints, the CPR never budged on the coal rate. This effectively ensured that the generally fine coal of the Nicola Valley mines was sold directly to the CPR for locomotive fuel, rather than be consigned to the coast for further sale. In 1912 the CPR started converting many mainline steam locomotives to oil fuel, and had the First World War not created an oil shortage the market for Merritt coal might have been totally lost.

Despite the CPR monopoly, the Nicola Valley prospered as a result of its railway. And true to Shaughnessy's earlier promise, the CPR rail line in the Nicola Valley was extended through to Midway. This work was carried out by its subsidiary Kettle Valley Railway, after the CPR secured the charter of the original railway centred in Grand Forks. In 1915 the Nicola Branch was formally transferred to the Kettle Valley Railway. Thereafter, it was an integral part of "The KV."

FIGURE 3-4

Time Table No. 10, June 2nd, 1907.

NORTHBOUND TRAINS Inferior direction.				NICOLA BRANCH			SOUTHBOUND TRAINS Superior direction.	
Second Class	Miles from Nicola	Telegraph Stations			Telegraph Calls		Second Class	
17 Tues. Thur. *Sat.				STATIONS.			16 Mon. Wed. *Fri.	
9.00	.0	D		Nicola	W	N A	18.00	
				7.0				
f 9.20	7.0			Merritt			f 17.41	
				2.0				
s 9.35	9.0			Coutlee			s 17.35	
				3.0				
s 9.45	12.0			Coyle			s 17.20	
				5.0				
s 10.00	17.0			Canford			s 17.05	
				4.0				
10.12	21.0			Water Tank	W		16.53	
				6.0				
s 10.30	27.0			Dot			s 16.35	
				5.0				
10.50	32.0			Water Tank	W		16.15	
				5.0				
f 11.10	37.0			Clapperton			f 15.55	
				3.0				
11.22	40.0			Water Tank	W		15.43	
				7.0				
11.45	47.0	D N		Spences Bridge Jct.	W	R N	15.15	
Tues. Thur. *Sat. 17							Mon. Wed. *Fri. 16	

Registering and Bulletin Points } Spences Bridge Jct. and Nicola.

Comparison Clock at Spences Bridge Jct.

FIGURE 3-5

FIGURE 3-6

◁ FIGURE 3-5 *When the Nicola Branch was completed the dominant community along the line was Nicola, at the end of track. However, Merritt quickly outgrew Nicola because of the presence of coal fields adjacent to the Coldwater River. The rapid rise of Merritt necessitated the temporary use of this boxcar for a station until a more permanent station could be built. The station opened in 1910, to be replaced by yet a larger one in 1912 as the community growth continued.* COLLECTION OF BARRIE SANFORD

◁ FIGURE 3-6 *Although coal attracted the railway to the Nicola Valley the cattle industry was also of importance to the railway. In the fall trains as long as 30 cars of cattle at a time left the Nicola Valley for the Vancouver market. Most cattle were loaded at Nicola. This smaller corral at Merritt was built in 1912.* COLLECTION OF BARRIE SANFORD

▽ FIGURE 3-7 *Although this photo cannot be identified with certainty, the author believes that it was taken in the Nicola Valley early in January 1907. The men posing for the picture had come by special train from Vancouver to tour the Nicola Valley Coal & Coke Company mine, then nearing completion. The Nicola Herald reported that the men were taken by sleigh to tour the mine.* CITY OF VANCOUVER ARCHIVES (N872 P49)

FIGURE 3-7

FIGURE 3-8

△ FIGURE 3-8 *This narrow gauge locomotive — nicknamed "The Dinky" — was used to haul coal from the Nicola Valley Coal & Coke Company's Number Two mine to the main loading tipple. At the tipple coal would be loaded into open hopper cars or boxcars with interior wooden doors for shipment. The Middlesboro mine was the CPR's most important customer on the Nicola Branch. The relationship was mutual, as the CPR was the mine's best customer.* COLLECTION OF BARRIE SANFORD

▽ FIGURE 3-9 *Middlesboro Collieries of the Nicola Valley Coal & Coke Company across the Coldwater River from Merritt. This was the largest coal mine in the Nicola Valley. It commenced shipping coal in 1907 and remained in operation until 1944.* COLLECTION OF BARRIE SANFORD

FIGURE 3-9

▽ FIGURE 3-10 *Coal from the Merritt mine supplied this coal chute at Spences Bridge, where the Nicola Branch joined the CPR mainline, as well as several others on the CPR system. Cars loaded with coal would be run up the incline on the right, and the coal unloaded into a pit from where it would be conveyed by elevators to the upper bins. It could then be poured quickly into locomotive tenders during station stops. After the last Merritt mine closed in 1944 coal from Michel was used until the final exit of steam from the CPR in the province in 1957. This particular chute survived another nine years, being demolished in November 1966.* PHOTO BY BARRIE SANFORD

FIGURE 3-10

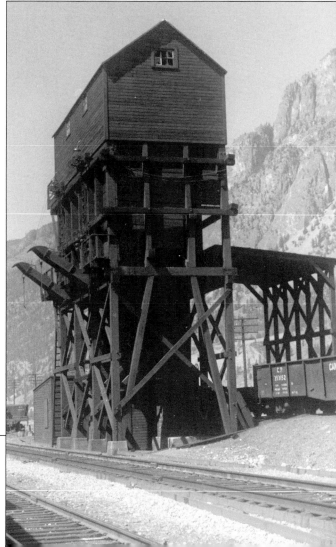

Kettle Valley Railway Dateline

Nicola Branch

1891-04-20	British Columbia government granted charter for Nicola, Kamloops & Similkameen Coal & Railway Company and Nicola Valley Railway.
1894-04-17	First sod turned on Nicola Valley Railway at Spences Bridge. No further work done.
1905-05-16	CPR announced that contract for construction of line between Spences Bridge and Nicola let to Loss, Macdonell & Company.
1905-06-20	Construction commenced.
1905-11-16	NK&S leased to CPR for "999 years."
1906-01-08	Tracklaying commenced at Spences Bridge.
1906-03-19	First train passed through "Ten Mile Hill" tunnel at Clapperton.
1906-06-07	Tracklaying reached Coutlee.
1906-10-31	Railway Commission approved line between Spences Bridge and Coutlee for regular operation. Limited freight service introduced.
1906-11-02	Tracklaying completed at Nicola.
1907-01-22	First car of coal shipped from Nicola Valley.
1907-02-07	Railway Commission approved line between Coutlee and Nicola for regular operation.
1907-04-01	Nicola Branch officially opened. First regular train delayed until April 3 owing to washout on opening day. Service was mixed train three times per week.
1910-02-07*	First station at Merritt opened, replacing boxcar.
1910-04-11	Mixed train service changed to daily except Sunday.
1911-03-04	Six freight cars and three passenger cars of westbound mixed train derailed at Clapperton.
1911-06-05	Separate passenger and freight train service introduced, replacing mixed train. Passenger service seven days per week.
1911-08-04	Nicola Valley Pine Lumber Company shipped first car of lumber from Canford Mill.
1912-06-06	Nicola enginehouse destroyed by fire.
1912-07-26	Seven dump cars and ballast plow destroyed in derailment at Coutlee after running loose from Merritt yard.
1912-09-06*	Second station at Merritt opened.
1912-11-21	Log train backed into log pond at Canford Mills. One killed.
1913-11-22	Sunday passenger train service discontinued.
1915-10-31	Nicola Branch taken over by Kettle Valley Railway.

△ FIGURE 3-11 *The lumber industry ultimately usurped coal as the dominant industry of the Nicola Valley. This picture was taken in the Coldwater Valley above Merritt in 1913 on the Kettle Valley Railway. CPR engine 3000 and her cars of logs are destined for the Nicola Valley Lumber Company mill on the Nicola Branch at Canford. Teams of horses have brought logs from the bush and stacked them alongside the track for loading onto railcars. The Nicola Valley Lumber Company — later Nicola Pine Mills — was a pioneer in the cutting and export of interior pine, considered by many at the time to be economically worthless.*
COLLECTION OF BARRIE SANFORD

^cCulloch's Wonder

Construction of the Midway-Merritt line

THE OPENING YEARS OF THE TWENTIETH CENTURY WIDENED AND INTENSIFIED THE COMPETITIVE RIVALRY between the Canadian Pacific Railway and Great Northern Railway in southern British Columbia. Hill's line up the Kettle River into Grand Forks and Phoenix secured the major share of the Boundary District ore trade away from the CPR. His line into Crowsnest Pass was also directly connected with the GN mainline, offering a through route on easy grades for Fernie coal from the East Kootenays to reach the Grand Forks smelter. By contrast, the CPR faced steep grades on the line west of Robson and had still to rely on water connections to link its Boundary and West Kootenay rail segments with the rest of its system. Not content with this savagery of the CPR, Hill announced in December 1904 that he would immediately start construction of a rail line along the Kettle River from Curlew west to the coast. Hill's engineers were soon in the Hope Mountains retracing the survey lines cut by the Dewdney Expedition four years earlier.

On May 24, 1905 Hill awarded the first contract on his projected railway westward from Curlew. Construction also began eastward from the coast towards a meeting point in the Hope Mountains. A sharp economic downturn in the latter half of the decade slowed progress, but by the end of 1909 Great Northern track stretched from Vancouver east to Abbotsford, and from the Kootenay and Boundary district up the Similkameen Valley to Princeton. Early in 1910 contracts were awarded for additional sections eastward to Hope and westward to Coalmont. An eight-mile-long tunnel under the Hope Mountains was proposed to help close the intervening 40-mile gap.

For the Canadian Pacific Railway the situation was now critical. Its tenuous position in the Kootenays and the Boundary District would likely be eradicated if the Great Northern completed a railway across the Hope Mountains. Hill had already captured most of the freight traffic in southern British Columbia. A direct railway to the coast would allow him to secure all that remained. The CPR, with a much longer route from the Kootenays to either tidewater or a Canadian centre equivalent in commercial stature to Spokane — and still dependent upon boat connections — would be driven from southern British Columbia.

CPR President Thomas Shaughnessy believed that the CPR had to construct

◁ FIGURE 4-1
Construction of the Kettle Valley Railway involved many engineering challenges, but Chief Engineer Andrew McCulloch handled the task so skillfully that the railway was soon dubbed ''McCulloch's Wonder'' by McCulloch's assistant engineers. One such challenge was the major bridge across Trout Creek, just west of Penticton. In this photo a wooden falsework trestle can be seen reaching up from the creekbed to support the steel truss span during its construction.
PENTICTON MUSEUM (37-783)

◁ FIGURE 4-2 *Annual Pass on the Kettle Valley Railway issued to Andrew McCulloch.* COURTESY ANDREW McCULLOCH FOUNDATION

its own Coast-to-Kootenay rail line if the company's existing investment in southern British Columbia was to be protected. He struck an alliance with James John Warren, an Ontario barrister who was manager of the Trusts & Guarantee Company, the backer of the Kettle River Valley Railway's ill-fated enterprise at Grand Forks. An arrangement was committed whereby the Kettle Valley Railway, with Warren as president, would build from Midway to Merritt and across the Hope Mountains to Hope. The CPR would finance construction in return for the securities of the smaller company. Although the use of a subsidiary company for railway expansion was not unusual for Canadian Pacific, Shaughnessy gave the Kettle Valley Railway a degree of independence unknown by other corporate affiliates.

Shaughnessy gave the Kettle Valley Railway one thing more: Andrew McCulloch. Shaughnessy chose as the chief engineer of the Kettle Valley Railway a man who had been involved with nearly every CPR line in southern British Columbia and many lines in other parts of the United States and Canada, including the famed Spiral Tunnels on the CPR mainline. Shaughnessy recognized that construction of 350 miles of railway across three major mountain ranges, including rugged Coquihalla Pass through the Hope Mountains, demanded an engineer of tremendous talent. He could hardly have chosen better than Andrew McCulloch.

Late in May 1910 Warren and McCulloch were introduced. The two men reviewed the earlier surveys and the general directives which Shaughnessy had given each of them. They decided to route the railway from Midway along the Kettle River and its West Fork to the 4150-foot-high pass at Hydraulic Summit, a location later named McCulloch in honour of the chief engineer's remarkable work in building the KVR. From that point the line would descend along the mountainside east of Okanagan Lake to Penticton. After leaving Penticton the line would climb northwest up the

▽ FIGURE 4-3 *The Kettle Valley Railway builders: James Warren and Andrew McCulloch. The date and location of the photograph is unknown, but it was probably taken a few years after completion of the KVR during one of their many exploration journeys together.* COURTESY ANDREW McCULLOCH FOUNDATION

valley of Trout Creek to Osprey Lake, and route overland to Brookmere, at that time called Otter Summit. From a point just west of there the line would split. One line would descend the valley of the Coldwater River to the existing CPR line at Merritt. A second line — nominally a branch line though in fact the KVR mainline — would head southwest through Coquihalla Pass to Hope.

The task was immense. Besides the obvious engineering and construction difficulties, Canada was in a period of unprecedented prosperity. Construction materials were in short supply. Labour was hard to obtain. Locomotives and freight cars were practically nonexistent. The shortages of manpower and materials slowed the pace of construction below that originally hoped for in the race against Hill. However, the railway was remarkably well built. Within two years of the start of construction the awed assistant engineers working under Andrew McCulloch had dubbed the new railway ''McCulloch's Wonder.''

FIGURE 4-3

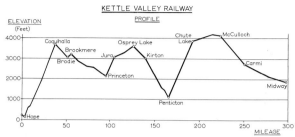

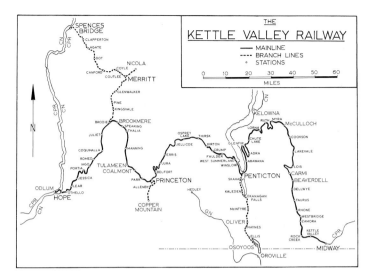

The adjacent map shows the circuitous routing of the Kettle Valley Railway made necessary by the north-south alignment of mountain ranges and intervening river valleys which ran transverse to the east-west objectives of the railway. The profile shows the resulting grades, which one reflective locomotive fireman said ".. . ranged from 2.2% to steep." Ruling grades of 2.0% or over were in effect on 100 miles of the 300 miles of trackage between Midway and Hope. Small wonder firemen on hand-fired steam locomotives found the railway difficult!

Others were impressed too. When the provincial government inspector examined the line between Merritt and Brookmere in November 1911, the newspaper covering his report stated: "He pronounced it to be the best section of railway he had ever examined, thus reflecting great credit on the engineering staff of the railway company."[6]

Much credit for the railway's construction also goes to the common labourers, employed by the thousands in that age before extensive mechanization. Compressed-air drills were available for drilling blasting holes and steam shovels were used for excavating some earth cuts. But the bulk of the work of construction was performed using human and animal muscle. The labourers came from all over the world, although most were new immigrants from central Europe who came to Canada specifically to engage in railway construction work. A few patriotic individuals returned home at the outbreak of the First World War, but most remained in Canada and became solid Canadian citizens. Contrary to popular myth, alcohol, gambling and prostitution were not significant problems among the labourers. As one former labourer said to the author, "All that went on in those days was work, work, work!" At the peak of KVR construction more than 5000 labourers were at work on the railway. Taking into account manpower turnover, perhaps 15,000 men altogether worked on building "The KV."

Penticton was selected as the location for the KVR headquarters, and a station, roundhouse and shop facilities were constructed. The station was built adjacent to the wharf on Okanagan Lake to provide convenient connections between KVR trains and the CPR lakeboats. The lakeshore station was designated "Penticton" and was reached by a 1.8-mile-long spur from the main railway yard, shops and roundhouse at "South Penticton." In 1941, after CPR passenger service on Okanagan Lake had been discontinued a new station was built at the railway yard and it adopted the Penticton name. The company also built a major hotel — the Incola — in anticipation that the scenic wonders along the railway would attract a large tourist trade, similar to that enjoyed by the CPR in the Rocky Mountains.

△ FIGURE 4-4
Penticton Reeve E. Foley-Bennett addresses a Dominion Day gathering on July 1, 1911 prior to turning the first official sod on Kettle Valley Railway construction at Penticton. Construction had already started from the ends of CPR trackage at Merritt and Midway, but Penticton was a logical point from which to also construct the railway because of the ease with which supplies could be delivered by barge from Okanagan Landing. PENTICTON MUSEUM (37-3304)

By the end of 1913 track had been laid on more than half the railway, and much of the remainder was under contract for construction. However, economic conditions began to sag badly in 1913, then in August 1914 the First World War began. As a consequence the CPR and GN tempered their rivalry considerably, and it was agreed that the KVR and VV&E would share trackage west of Princeton. Two agreements were signed between the parties. The ''Coquihalla Agreement,'' as it became commonly known, governed the sharing of KVR track between Hope and Brookmere. The ''Tulameen Agreement'' governed the sharing of VV&E tracks between Brookmere and Princeton. Thus the KVR did not build between Princeton and Brookmere, but simply operated its trains over the trackage which the VV&E completed between the two points in 1914.

The KVR was formally linked with the VV&E at Princeton in a modest ceremony on April 23, 1915, at which the wife of the local minister drove the final spike. Another month was needed to ballast and trim the new track. On May 31, 1915 the Kettle Valley Railway line between Midway and Merritt was officially opened and a celebration banquet held at Penticton, with invited guests coming from all across southern British Columbia.

Passenger service was at first very modest, owing in part to the effects of the war. Service was limited to a mixed train, three times per week, with a night layover at Penticton. A change of trains was also required at Merritt, since that was the junction point with the CPR at the west end of the line. Service improved somewhat later in 1915 when the CPR turned over the Nicola Branch to the CPR. However, the Kettle Valley Railway would have to await the opening of the line through Coquihalla Pass the following year before effectively completing the Coast-to-Kootenay railway.

Kettle Valley Railway Dateline

General
1909-1915

1909-11-25	Richard McBride re-elected premier of British Columbia on a platform of railway aid, including a cash subsidy of $5000 per mile for the KVR line between Merritt and Penticton.
1910-06-21	KVR announced that Penticton would be made the headquarters of the KVR.
1912-03-08	Richard McBride re-elected premier of British Columbia on a platform of railway aid, including a cash subsidy of $10,000 per mile for the KVR line through Coquihalla Pass and $200,000 for a bridge across the Fraser River at Hope.
1912-08-16	KVR Incola Hotel at Penticton opened.
1913-07-01	KVR leased to CPR for 999 years.
1915-05-31	KVR officially opened. Tri-weekly mixed train service commenced between Merritt and Midway.
1915-10-31	KVR took over CPR Nicola Branch. Mixed trains operated through to Spences Bridge.

▽ FIGURE 4-5 *Kettle Valley Railway locomotive No. 2. This engine was the second of two identical 4-6-0's built by Alco in June 1904 (Serial Numbers 29786 and 29787) for the Newton & Northwestern Railway and sold to the KVR in 1912 where they became No. 1 and No. 2. The KVR had two other locomotives bearing the Kettle Valley Railway name, in addition to the three locomotives based at Grand Forks. All other locomotives used on the line were leased from the CPR and bore the Canadian Pacific name.*
COLLECTION OF
BARRIE SANFORD

FIGURE 4-5

Kettle Valley Railway Dateline

Construction Merritt-Brookmere

1910-06-30   Contract for construction of 30 miles of line between Merritt and Brookmere awarded to Macdonnell, Gzowski & Company.

1910-07-09   Construction started at Merritt.

1910-10-25   First spike ceremony held at Merritt.

1910-12-18   First locomotive arrived at Merritt.

1910-12-19   Tracklaying started at Merritt. (Token amount of track had been laid a few days earlier.)

1911-09-29   Track reached Brookmere.

1912-06-23   Engine 131 operated picnic excursion from Merritt to Glenwalker and return. This was the first passenger train on the Merritt-Midway line.

1912-10-07   Railway Commission approved line between Merritt and Brookmere for regular operation.

▽ FIGURE 4-6
Crossties for the new rail line up the Coldwater Valley are seen stockpiled at the south end of the rail yard in Merritt in the spring of 1911. A pack train of supplies is also readying to set out for up the line. COURTESY ANDREW McCULLOCH FOUNDATION

FIGURE 4-6

△ FIGURE 4-7 *The Kettle Valley Railway was constructed in an age before extensive mechanization, and most work had to be done by human or animal labour. This light "tramway" track was used by horse-drawn carts carrying rock from the cut after the rock had been broken by blasting. The engineers would try to locate the railway to balance adjacent excavations and fills so that minimum earth and rock movement was required to complete an even roadbed for the track.*

Long sections of the railway were contracted to major construction firms, which often in turn sublet sections of the work to smaller contracting firms. The subcontractors employed labourers directly or sublet "stations." A "station" represented 100 feet of right-of-way, and the contract for this would be taken by one man or a small group of men who tented on the site and worked independently. For "stationmen" the attraction was potentially greater earnings than through direct employment, where wages generally were about $2.75 per day, with deductions for board and medical care. However, the risk was considerable. If the work was harder than anticipated a "stationman" could have little profit or lose heavily after paying expenses. PENTICTON MUSEUM (37-783: NEG. 1808A)

FIGURE 4-8

▷ FIGURE 4-8 *The line between Midway and Penticton was not given a name in the first timetable issued by the KVR in 1915. In 1916 it was named First District, but in 1921 became the Carmi Subdivision, which name it retained until the line's abandonment. Note that in this extract from an early timetable the Carmi Subdivision extends beyond the South Penticton yard to the lakeshore station.*
COLLECTION OF
BARRIE SANFORD

Miles from Midway	Telegraph and Telephone Offices	CARMI SUBDIVISION STATIONS	Telegraph Calls	Car Capacity Passing Tracks
.0	D N	MIDWAY ZK	M I	
8.8	Z ★	8.8 KETTLE VALLEY Z		
11.7	D	2.9 ROCK CREEK ZR	K	38
18.9		7.2 ZAMORA		36
20.5	Z ★	1.6 WESTBRIDGE ZW		
24.8		4.3 RHONE		37
31.4		6.6 TAURUS		37
35.9	Z ★	4.5 ZW		
42.3		6.4 BEAVERDELL		33
46.6	Z	4.3 CARMI ZCW		23
54.2		7.6 LOIS		27
61.0		6.8 LAKEVALE ZW		38
69.3		8.3 COOKSON		27
76.6	Z	7.3 McCULLOCH ZYW		51
83.9		7.3 MYRA		37
86.6	Z ★	2.7 ZW		
91.2		4.6 RUTH		43
96.6	Z ★	5.4 ZW		
97.6		1.0 LORNA		33
106.5	Z	8.9 CHUTE LAKE ZYW		37
113.2	Z	6.7 ADRA W		25
118.9		5.7 GLENFIR		26
125.7	Z	6.8 ARAWANA W		40
129.1		3.4 ★ POPLAR GROVE		
133.6	D N Z	4.5 SOUTH PENTICTON YK	S	37
135.4		1.8 PENTICTON	P N	

★No Passing Track

▷ FIGURES 4-10, 4-11, 4-12 *On the 3000-foot climb from Penticton to Chute Lake McCulloch employed a giant loop and spiral tunnel to keep the ruling grade at 2.2%. Even with these features 27 miles of such heavy grade were required. FIGURE 4-10 shows rock spoil being moved from the west portal of the 1604-foot-long spiral tunnel at the apex of the upper loop. This tunnel — known as Adra Tunnel or "Big Tunnel" — was at Mile 113.9 (Carmi Subdivision) and was the longest tunnel on the KVR. FIGURE 4-11 shows a nearby cut. FIGURE 4-12 shows the completed track on the lower loop at Glenfir. The loop and tunnel helped make this section of railway a scenic delight as well as an engineering marvel.* FIGURE 4-10 PROVINCIAL ARCHIVES OF BRITISH COLUMBIA (52469) FIGURE 4-11 PENTICTON MUSEUM (37-783; NEG. 574) FIGURE 4-12 COURTESY CANADIAN PACIFIC CORPORATE ARCHIVES

▽ FIGURE 4-9 *A blast ignites. Dynamite was only just starting to be used when the KVR was built. Prior to this black powder was the sole form of explosive available for the railway builders. Unlike black powder, which was usable at low temperatures, the nitroglycerine in dynamite froze readily under Canadian winter conditions, and workers occasionally heated the dynamite in frying pans or next to an open fire to thaw it for use. Numerous fatalities resulted. Such actions by the workers would seem almost unbelievable were the deaths not so well documented.* PENTICTON MUSEUM (37-783; NEG. 1808B)

FIGURE 4-9

FIGURE 4-10

FIGURE 4-11

FIGURE 4-12

MYRA

△ FIGURE 4-13 *Between Myra and Ruth — an area now commonly known as Myra Canyon — the twin forks of Canyon Creek forced the railway to wind into the canyon on a wide detour. This view of the west mileboard for Myra shows the trestle at Mile 85.2 (Carmi Subdivision) in the foreground, while across the canyon to the left is the trestle at Mile 90.4, more than five miles west by rail. The table on the opposite page lists the many tunnels and trestles in Myra Canyon.* PHOTO BY BARRIE SANFORD

▷ FIGURE 4-14 *This picture shows the tunnel at Mile 84.7 during the initial stages of construction. The tunnel was significant in that it was never completed. Loose rock encountered near the centre of the tunnel resulted in a decision being made to excavate a deep cut instead.* PENTICTON MUSEUM

FIGURE 4-14

FIG

FIGURE 4-15

△ FIGURE 4-15 *This view is looking eastward along the railway from above the tunnel at Mile 85.7. The trestle at the bottom of the picture is the 80-foot-long trestle at Mile 85.6. In the distance the next four trestles east of that point are visible.* COLLECTION OF BARRIE SANFORD

Myra Canyon

MILE	FEATURE
84.0	MYRA: Passing Track
84.9	Frame Trestle: 180 feet long
85.2	Frame Trestle: 90 feet long
85.25	Frame Trestle: 90 feet long
85.3	Frame Trestle: 145 feet long
85.35	Frame Trestle: 240 feet long
85.45	Frame Trestle: 285 feet long
85.6	Frame Trestle: 80 feet long
85.7	Tunnel: 375 feet long
85.9	Frame Trestle: 434 feet long
86.2	Tunnel: 277 feet long
86.4	Frame Trestle: 194 feet long
86.5	East Fork Canyon Creek Bridge: Five steel through plate girder spans on steel towers: 365 feet long, 158 feet high. Originally frame trestle.
86.55	Frame Trestle: 240 feet long
87.4	Frame Trestle: 300 feet long
87.9	West Fork Canyon Creek Bridge: Twelve steel through plate girder spans on steel towers: 721 feet long, 182 feet high. Originally frame trestle.
88.0	Frame Trestle: 75 feet long
88.2	Frame Trestle: 429 feet long
88.4	Frame Trestle: 270 feet long
89.4	Frame Trestle: 360 feet long
90.4	Frame Trestle: 256 feet long
91.2	RUTH: Passing Track

This data is from the CPR 1947 Kettle Valley Division Engineering Data Book which accurately reflects the trestles and tunnels that can still be found by hiking the abandoned line. At the time of the line's construction there were several additional trestles. These were filled in prior to 1947.

FIGURE 4-16

FIGURES 4-16, 4-17, 4-18 *Well known photographer G.H. Hudson took this remarkable panoramic view photograph of the east half of Myra Canyon from a position just east of the trestle at Mile 86.9 (detail FIGURE 4-17). This particular trestle does not show in the table on the previous page as it was filled in during 1929. The trestle on the extreme left across the canyon in FIGURE 4-16 is at Mile 85.2. The trestle on the extreme right is the one over East Fork Canyon Creek at Mile 86.5 (detail FIGURE 4-18). The trestle which appears immediately across East Fork from the photographer's location (FIGURE 4-16) is the 194-foot-long trestle at Mile 86.4, which is just west of the highest point on the entire Kettle Valley Railway — 4178 feet. The condition of the track and the absence of telegraph lines in the picture indicates that the railway has not yet opened for operation.*

FIGURE 4-17

FIGURE 4-16

The notations on the upper left part of the photograph are by Andrew McCulloch. For those who can read his fine writing, the mileage and trestle count is based westward from McCulloch station. There was one trestle between McCulloch and Myra, hence he has labelled the first trestle in Myra Canyon Trestle No. 2.

Construction of these wooden trestles was no minor feat. Each timber member had to be cut and bored by hand, using a team of more than 50 carpenters stationed in a framing yard at Carmi. No shims were permitted; fitting had to be exact. The total amount of timber in these trestles is not known, but more than 25 cars of bridge bolts were required. COURTESY ANDREW McCULLOCH FOUNDATION

FIGURE 4-18

▷ FIGURE 4-19 *This photo taken in January 1914 shows tracklaying work just east of Penticton as crews push rails eastward to a meeting point with the track from Midway. Ties and rails are fed forward from the flat cars and loosely spiked into place. The tracklaying train then proceeds forward a rail length and the next rail is laid. Note the few spikes in the track in the foreground. After the rails have been spiked, gravel ballast will be poured over the ties to stabilize them.* PENTICTON MUSEUM (37-3304; NEG. 263)

Kettle Valley Railway Dateline

Construction Midway-Penticton

1910-08-10	KVR announced contract for construction of 35 miles of line westward from Midway awarded to L.M. Rice & Company.
1910-10-04	Construction started at Midway.
1911-01-17	Tracklaying started at Midway.
1911-07-12	KVR announced L.M. Rice & Company had been awarded a contract for construction of additional 40 miles of line to McCulloch.
1912-08-03	KVR announced contract for construction of 57 miles of line between McCulloch and Penticton awarded to Grant Smith & Company.
1912-09-16	First train reached Carmi.
1912-10-07	Railway Commission approved line between Midway and Carmi for regular operation.
1912-10-24	Grading eastward from Penticton started.
1914-02-03	Railway Commission approved line between Carmi and McCulloch for regular operation.
1914-03-29	Excursion train operated from Penticton to Little Tunnel and return for Penticton citizens.
1914-08-19	Excursion train operated from Penticton to Adra Tunnel and return for delegates of the Western Canada Irrigation Association convention.
1914-10-02	Last spike on line between Midway and Penticton driven at Mile 87.9 (Carmi Subdivision).
1914-10-06	First train from Midway arrived at Penticton.
1914-10-16	Railway Commission approved line between McCulloch and Penticton for regular operation.

FIGURE 4-20

FIGURES 4-20 & 4-21 *For three days in August 1914 the Western Canada Irrigation Association held its annual convention in Penticton. On August 19 the KVR outfitted three flatcars with seats and pushed the cars from Penticton up to Adra Tunnel to give delegates a view of the Kettle Valley Railway east of Penticton, then nearly completed. FIGURE 4-20 shows the ladies of the group posing at the west portal of the tunnel. FIGURE 4-21 shows the train just to the west of the site of the earlier photograph.* COLLECTION OF BARRIE SANFORD

FIGURE 4-21

FIGURE 4-22

△ FIGURE 4-22 *West of Penticton a major obstacle to the railway's progress was posed by Trout Creek, which cut a deep canyon in its plunge to Okanagan Lake. When McCulloch first proposed keeping the KVR on the south side of Trout Creek canyon the* Summerland Review *objected, stating that crossing the creek required only an "infinitesimal" bridge. After several options were considered a decision was made to cross the canyon with a 241-foot-high deck truss bridge, the highest bridge on the KVR. FIGURE 4-22 shows the wooden trestles on the approaches to the main steel span prior to the start of steel placement.*

Murdock McKay, a KVR locomotive engineer who had joined the company in 1911 as an assistant to Andrew McCulloch, fondly remembered McCulloch's talents in the construction of this bridge. McCulloch had disputed with the engineers of the company erecting the steelwork concerning the computation of a certain bridge dimension. McCulloch, with McKay assisting him, took a surveying transit and steel measuring tape and resurveyed the entire canyon terrain. McKay said that he was barely able to keep up with McCulloch, then a man nearly 50 years of age. Afterwards McCulloch stayed up all night to complete his calculations from the field notes. McKay recalled watching as the final piece of the 250-foot-long main span was placed — a piece which was only one-quarter of an inch short of being a perfect fit. It was an amazing memory of an amazing man! PENTICTON MUSEUM (37-783)

FIGURE 4-23

Miles from Penticton	Telegraph and Telephone Offices	PRINCETON SUBDIVISION STATIONS	Telegraph Calls	Car Capacity Passing Tracks
.0	D N Z	PENTICTON ZYK Jct. Osoyoos S.D.	S	
		7.0		
7.0		WINSLOW Z		35
		2.5		
9.5	D	WEST SUMMERLAND ZW W S		24
		6.0		
15.5		FAULDER		32
		5.0		
20.5	Z ★	W		
		5.2		
25.7	Z	KIRTON ZY		35
		3.8		
29.5	Z ★	W		
		2.9		
32.4		THIRSK		34
		6.1		
38.5	Z	OSPREY LAKE W		35
		7.2		
45.7		JELLICOE		35
		4.5		
50.2	Z ★	ZW		
		3.1		
53.3		ERRIS		35
		6.8		
60.1	Z	JURA YW		33
		5.1		
65.2		BELFORT		40
		5.3		
70.5	D N Z	PRINCETON ZYWCB O D Jct. Copper Mountain S.D.		46
		11.7		
82.2		COALMONT Z		39
		4.0		
86.2		TULAMEEN ZW		44
		6.8		
93.0		MANNING		57
		10.0		
103.0		THALIA		26
		2.0		
105.0		SPEARING		56
		3.6		
108.6	D N Z	BROOKMERE K B R		

★ No Passing Track

◁ FIGURE 4-23 *The line between Penticton and Brookmere was named the Princeton Subdivision. On the section between Princeton and Brookmere Great Northern mileages were used until 1945, when the GN sold the trackage to the CPR. The symbol W indicates water tank.* COLLECTION OF BARRIE SANFORD

▽ FIGURE 4-24 *The completed bridge at Trout Creek viewed from the north bank of the creek downstream of the bridge. The wooden approach trestles were replaced by steel structures and fills in 1927-28.* COLLECTION OF BARRIE SANFORD

FIGURE 4-24

FIGURE 4-25

△ FIGURE 4-25
*Siwash Creek
trestle, Mile 48.4
(Princeton Subdivision),
viewed from the east end
in early 1915 prior to
tracklaying. This
785-foot-long frame
trestle originally had a
short plate girder span
at the centre. The trestle
was later rebuilt without
the girder span and was
replaced by a fill in
1947-48.* COLLECTION OF
BARRIE SANFORD

▷ FIGURE 4-26 *Crews at
work on the west face of
Erris Tunnel at Mile 54.7
(Princeton Subdivision). The
crews digging the 300-foot-long
tunnel are using the "English"
method of tunnel construction in
which both a "heading," at the
crown of the tunnel, and a
"drift" at the bottom have been
driven. Much of this tunnel was
through loose rock and had to be
braced with wooden timbers as
excavation proceeded. The timber
lining was still in place when
train service over the line ceased
in 1989, making it one of the
last timber-lined tunnels to be
in use on the CPR system.*
PENTICTON MUSEUM (37-2838;
NEG. 2620D)

FIGURE 4-26

FIGURE 4-27 BRITISH COLUMBIA MAPS

FIGURES 4-27, 4-28, 4-29 *The 1912 decision to route the KVR mainline via Princeton instead of the originally planned route via Aspen Grove forced the railway to make an abrupt descent from high on the valley of Five Mile Creek down into Princeton. McCulloch chose to maintain a 2.2% grade by laying out three remarkable loops on the open rangeland northeast of Princeton. The station at the bottom of the first loop was named Belfort, after the famous French garrison in the Jura Mountains which resisted the German invasion of 1870. The station at the top of the upper loop was named Jura. FIGURE 4-27 is an aerial view of the loops. FIGURE 4-28 shows a train of rails and ties descending the grade at Mile 64. FIGURE 4-29 shows the same train at Mile 63.*

FIGURE 4-28 PROVINCIAL ARCHIVES OF BRITISH COLUMBIA (52467)

FIGURE 4-29 PROVINCIAL ARCHIVES OF BRITISH COLUMBIA (52477)

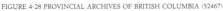

Kettle Valley Railway Dateline

Construction Penticton-Princeton

1911-06-10	First pile driven on KVR wharf at Penticton.
1911-07-01	Official sod turning at Penticton.
1911-10-30*	Contract for construction of first portion of line westward from Penticton awarded to L.M. Rice & Company. Company subsequently awarded contract for remainder of line to Osprey Lake.
1911-12-11	First rail cars delivered to Penticton by barge.
1912-04-10	KVR announced railway mainline would be routed via Princeton rather than Aspen Grove as originally planned.
1912-10-26	First locomotive arrived at Penticton.
1913-05-10	Falsework of Trout Creek bridge washed out.
1913-10-25	First official train crossed Trout Creek bridge.
1913-12-10	Tracklaying completed to Osprey Lake.
1914-02-03	Railway Commission approved line between Penticton and Mile 17 for regular operation.
1914-03-13*	Contract for construction of 32 miles of line between Osprey Lake and Princeton awarded to Guthrie, McDougall & Company.
1914-09-15	Railway Commission approved line between Mile 17 and Osprey Lake for regular operation.
1915-03-16	Tracklaying started westward from Osprey Lake.
1915-04-21	Track reached Princeton.
1915-04-23	Last spike on Merritt-Midway line formally driven at Princeton.
1915-05-27	Railway Commission approved line between Osprey Lake and Princeton for regular operation.

FIGURE 4-30

FIGURE 4-31 COURTESY VINTAGE VISUALS (GNR016)

☐ FIGURES 4-31 & 4-32 *West of Princeton KVR trains operated over the tracks of the VV&E as far as Brookmere, where the VV&E joined onto the KVR line from Merritt in October 1914. FIGURE 4-31 shows two small construction locomotives of contractor Guthrie, McDougall & Company at work grading the VV&E roadbed near Tulameen. The KVR's use of the track was permitted under the "Tulameen Agreement" (FIGURE 4-32) signed by both parties on July 10, 1914. After KVR trains commenced operation the Great Northern ran only a few trains as far west as Coalmont. Ultimately the trackage was sold to the CPR.*

FIGURE 4-32 COLLECTION OF BARRIE SANFORD

◁ FIGURE 4-30
Tracklaying on the Midway-Merritt line draws to a close on April 21, 1915 as KVR tracklaying crews approach the VV&E at Princeton. The view is looking westward, the photographer having used the VV&E truss bridge over the Similkameen River to secure a vantage point. The VV&E station and water tank are visible in the distance. The two-stall enginehouse is out of the picture beyond the station. The Great Northern, running trains on behalf of the VV&E, had commenced regular operations into Princeton on December 23, 1909. COLLECTION OF BARRIE SANFORD

Dated 10th day of July, 1914.

Vancouver, Victoria and Eastern Railway and Navigation Company

AND

The Kettle Valley Railway Company

AGREEMENT.

Kettle Valley Railway Dateline

VV&E Construction Princeton-Brookmere
(Line used by KVR)

1910-01-14	VV&E announced contract for construction of 18 miles of line between Princeton and Coalmont awarded to J.W. Stewart & Company.
1910-02-21	Construction started at Princeton on line westward to Coalmont.
1911-11-10	Track reached Coalmont from Princeton. Track was subsequently laid to a point a mile beyond Coalmont.
1912-02-18	Railway Commission approved VV&E line between Princeton and one mile beyond Coalmont for regular operation subject to completion of telegraph line.
1912-05-01	GN commenced regular twice per week train service between Princeton and Coalmont.
1912-09-20	VV&E announced that contract for construction of 42 miles of line from near Coalmont to Coquihalla awarded to Guthrie, McDougall & Company. Contract was subsequently cut back to Brookmere after agreement made with KVR.
1912-11-01*	Construction commenced westward from near Coalmont.
1914-07-10	KVR and VV&E formally signed Tulameen Agreement governing joint use of tracks Princeton-Brookmere.
1914-10-25	KVR and VV&E track joined at Brookmere.
1915-05-28	Railway Commission approved line between Coalmont and Brookmere for regular operation.

▷ FIGURES 4-33, 4-34, 4-35 *On May 31, 1915 regular train operations commenced on the Kettle Valley Railway between Midway and Merritt. FIGURE 4-33 shows Engine No. 4 at Penticton lakeshore station on that day with the first passenger train from Merritt. Later in the evening it would be joined by a train from Midway, after which a major celebration was held in the nearby Incola Hotel. FIGURE 4-34 shows the first timetable issued by the KVR. FIGURE 4-35 is Andrew McCulloch's invitation to the celebration banquet at Penticton.*

FIGURE 4-33 PENTICTON MUSEUM — STOCK'S FAMILY COLLECTION

FIGURE 4-34 COLLECTION OF DEAN OGLE

KETTLE VALLEY RAILWAY CO.

—

TIME 1 TABLE

TAKING EFFECT AT 24.01 O'CLOCK

SUNDAY, MAY 30, 1915

GOVERNED BY PACIFIC TIME

FOR THE INFORMATION AND GOVERNMENT OF EMPLOYES ONLY

—

THE SUPERIOR DIRECTION IS EAST OR SOUTH, AND EAST OR SOUTH BOUND TRAINS ARE SUPERIOR
TO TRAINS OF THE SAME CLASS IN THE OPPOSITE (INFERIOR) DIRECTION.

—

THE COMPANY'S RULES ARE PRINTED SEPARATELY IN BOOK FORM. EVERY EMPLOYEE WHOSE
DUTIES ARE PRESCRIBED BY THE RULES, AND EVERY EMPLOYEE WHOSE DUTIES ARE CONNECTED WITH
THE MOVEMENT OF TRAINS, MUST HAVE A COPY OF THE RULES AND OF THE CURRENT TIME TABLE
ACCESSIBLE WHEN ON DUTY.

O. E. FISHER,
SUPERINTENDENT

The Municipal Council
and
The Board of Trade of Penticton
Extends to
Mr. *Andrew McCulloch Esq*
An invitation to attend a Banquet at the
Incola Hotel, Penticton, B. C.
Monday evening, May thirty-first
To mark the arrival of the first trains on the
Kettle Valley Railway

Reception 8:15 p.m.   Banquet 8:45 p.m.   R. S. V. P.

Please send notice of acceptance to Secretary Penticton
Board of Trade, P. O. Box 442, Penticton, B. C., who will hand
name to head office Kettle Valley Railway Company to arrange free transportation.   Prompt acknowledgment requested.

FIGURE 4-35 COURTESY ANDREW McCULLOCH FOUNDATION

FIGURE 4-36

FIGURE 4-36 *On October 29, 1914 the staff of Penticton station posed for this picture on the eve of the departure of a number of the men to enlist in the armed forces following the outbreak of the First World War three months earlier. Seated: Andrew McCulloch and James Warren. Standing (left to right): Harold Burgess, W.J. Gibbons, Mr. Gann, Mr. Possie, Lindsay Swan, Reg McKenzie, Charles Gordon, W.V. Knox, Alex Swift, Mr. Osler, Mr. Graham, Vic Watson and Mr. Nicholl. Gordon was KVR secretary-treasurer. Swift was chief clerk.* COURTESY ANDREW McCULLOCH FOUNDATION

FIGURE 4-37 *Penticton citizens greatly enjoyed their new railway. On July 15, 1915 Engine No. 4 pulled a train with 530 Penticton residents on board up to Chute Lake for a day picnic. Here a group of the picnic party stand on the locomotive after it was turned on the wye and awaits the return to Penticton. It was a simple outing then; now the trip could not be made at any price.* PENTICTON MUSEUM (37-2986; NEG. 273-2)

FIGURE 4-37

FIGURE 4-38

△ FIGURE 4-38 *Not all early train rides on the Kettle Valley Railway were as festive as the picnic train on the previous page. This picture taken at Penticton on July 9, 1916 shows a special train which had just brought 519 men of the 225th Battalion (Kootenay) into Penticton from Nelson. The new recruits are transfering to the CPR steamer "Sicamous" for transport to the military training camp at Vernon. From there they were destined overseas to the killing fields of Europe. Almost certainly many of the young men in this photo would not return. The length of the train is uncertain, with varying reports between 11 and 13 cars. However, it was one of the longest passenger trains ever operated on the KVR.* PENTICTON MUSEUM

FIGURE 4-39

△ FIGURE 4-39 *Initially passenger service on the KVR was limited to mixed train operation. This picture was taken on board an eastbound mixed train crossing the large trestle across No Name Creek at Mile 52.7 (Princeton Subdivision), probably during the late summer of 1915 judging by the presence of the two empty cattle cars and a fruit reefer. The engine appears to be 3454, one of the early 2-8-0's leased to the KVR from the CPR. This trestle was replaced by a diversion and fill in 1928.* PROVINCIAL ARCHIVES OF BRITISH COLUMBIA (52470)

▷ FIGURE 4-40 *Kettle Valley Railway Engine No. 1 makes a dramatic pose at the east end of "Little Tunnel" at Mile 122 (Carmi Subdivision). The date is uncertain, but it has been suggested that the date is June 1, 1915, the day after regular train service on the Kettle Valley Railway commenced.* PENTICTON MUSEUM (37-783; NEG. 1810A)

ough Quarries

Construction of the Coquihalla line

THE MOST DIFFICULT SECTION OF THE KETTLE VALLEY
RAILWAY — AND THE SECTION WHICH ACCOUNTED FOR
much of the railway's reputation as a engineering marvel — was
the rail line through Coquihalla Pass. The 3646 foot summit of
Coquihalla Pass offered the lowest crossing of the Hope Mountains, making the pass
critical to the strategic railway situation in British Columbia. The Great Northern had
already announced its intentions to route the VV&E directly across the Hope Mountains via Coquihalla Pass, or under them with an eight-mile tunnel if necessary. Should
it do so the CPR's roundabout route to the Boundary and Kootenay districts could
well be rendered totally unable to compete with the GN's direct route.

In Shaughnessy's mind Canadian Pacific could not take that chance. He committed the Coquihalla line to being an integral part of the Kettle Valley Railway. The
completed rail line brought to fruition the Coast-to-Kootenay railway dream, and it
served southern British Columbia handsomely as a tool of future economic development. But for the CPR the Coquihalla line would earn the reputation of being the
most economically unremunerative section of trackage in its entire system. Coquihalla Pass, to recall Alexander Mackenzie, offered "superlative difficulties."

Immediately after the announcement that the KVR, with CPR sponsorship, would
build a railway through Coquihalla Pass, the rivalry between the KVR and VV&E to
secure right-of-way through the pass became intense. But soon the rivalry moderated. The defeat of the Laurier government in Ottawa over the issue of trade reciprocity
with the United States late in 1911 caused the GN to lose interest in its Canadian
rail lines. As well, Jim Hill was no longer GN president and had less control over the
company's affairs. When business conditions began to slump in 1913 the GN effectively conceded the battle for Coquihalla Pass. That year the two companies signed
an understanding, known as the "Coquihalla Agreement," authorizing the KVR to
build a rail line from Brookmere to Hope, with the VV&E being extended the right
to run trains over the KVR track for an annual rental fee.

◁ FIGURE 5-1
*"Rough quarries,
rocks and hills whose
heads touch heaven."*
Shakespeare's words so
inspired Kettle Valley
Railway Chief Engineer
Andrew McCulloch that
he named the station
immediately east of this
location Othello in
honour of the Bard's
immortal work. Here the
bridge at Mile 49.7 and
Tunnel 12 at Mile 49.65
(Coquihalla Subdivision)
can be seen piercing the
"rocks and hills" of the
Coquihalla River
canyon. COURTESY
CANADIAN PACIFIC
CORPORATE ARCHIVES (M5700)

FIGURES 5-2 - 5-5
Four miles east of Hope the Kettle Valley Railway entered the canyon of the Coquihalla River. Earlier engineers had proposed a long tunnel under the ridge to the west to avoid the canyon. McCulloch chose to go straight through — literally — with a tangent alignment which entailed four tunnels and two intermediate bridges. One of the tunnels was ''daylighted'' on the north side, creating the illusion of two tunnels rather than one. As a result the four tunnels became known as the ''Quintette Tunnels.''

FIGURE 5-2 shows a wood and rope walkway along the base of the canyon for surveyors.

The agreement reduced the rivalry, but not the magnitude of the construction task. The 38 miles of railway between Hope and Coquihalla required 43 bridges, 12 tunnels and 15 snowsheds. The First World War added problems, restricting many needed supplies, especially explosives, and reducing available manpower. The war also caused a general price inflation. Costs averaged $136,000 per mile, five times the Canadian average for railway construction at the time. One mile near the summit exceeded $300,000. Some reports stated that it was the most expensive railroad in the world.

The railway was very nearly completed in the fall of 1915. Fierce storms — and an incredible 67-foot snowfall that winter — forced construction crews to abandon work in late December. Not until May had the snow melted sufficiently to allow work to resume. All spring snowplows were needed to keep the line open for work trains, a haunting premonition of what was in store for the Kettle Valley Railway in Coquihalla Pass in the years to come. When the repair work was completed an informal last spike ceremony was held near the east end of Ladner Creek bridge, midway through Coquihalla Pass, and on July 31, 1916 the Coquihalla Pass rail line was opened for operation. That same day daily through-passenger train service was inaugurated between Vancouver and Nelson. Coast and Kootenay were at last linked by rail.

On September 15, 1916 Thomas Shaughnessy rode over the Coquihalla line in a special train from Penticton to the coast in the company of Warren and McCulloch. He expressed himself ''greatly impressed'' by the high quality of the line's construction.[7] Shaughnessy predicted that the years ahead would reveal the wisdom of the railway's construction.

Twelve days later, another special train operated over the Coquihalla line, this one an eastbound Great Northern train from Vancouver to Princeton carrying GN President Louis Hill, son of Jim Hill, and a small party of other GN officials. It was a symbolic tribute to ''Empire Builder'' Jim Hill, who had died four months earlier. No other Great Northern trains would ever operate over the Coquihalla Pass rail line.

FIGURE 5-2 COLLECTION OF BARRIE SANFORD

FIGURE 5-4

FIGURE 5-4 *Ladders used by workers during preliminary stages of construction. Blasters would have to light their charges, then scamper up these ladders to be out of the canyon before the subsequent explosion.* COLLECTION OF BARRIE SANFORD

▽ FIGURE 5-3 *Coquihalla River canyon looking downstream from the point where the Mile 49.6 bridge was later built.* COLLECTION OF BARRIE SANFORD

▽ FIGURE 5-5 *Tunnel excavators pose at the east portal of Tunnel 13.* COLLECTION OF BARRIE SANFORD

FIGURE 5-5

Kettle Valley Railway Dateline

Construction Coquihalla Line

1912-08-08	KVR announced contract for construction of 14 miles of line between Brodie and Coquihalla awarded to Twohy Brothers.
1913-04-09	KVR and VV&E announced Coquihalla Agreement drafted governing joint use of tracks Hope-Coquihalla.
1913-08-06	KVR announced contract for construction of 36 miles of line between Hope and Coquihalla awarded to McArthur Brothers.
1913-08-27	McArthur Brothers commenced construction work on Coquihalla line contract.
1913-11-20	KVR and VV&E formally signed Coquihalla Agreement.
1914-02-11	Ice flowing down river knocked out 250 feet of falsework of Fraser River bridge at Hope.
1915-05-28	Railway Commission approved line between Brodie and Coquihalla for regular operation.
1915-09-22	Railway Commission approved line for operation for 8.5 miles east of junction with CPR near Hope.
1915-12-27	McCulloch ordered construction work on Coquihalla line stopped because of severe weather.
1916-07-27	Railway Commission approved Coquihalla line for regular operations.
1916-07-31	Coquihalla line officially opened. Daily passenger train service between Vancouver and Nelson introduced.
1916-09-15	CPR President Thomas Shaughnessy rode over line from Penticton to Hope.
1916-09-27	GN operated special train from Vancouver to Princeton with Louis Hill and other officials on board. This was the only GN train to run over the Coquihalla line.

▷ FIGURE 5-6 *A view from the west side of the Coquihalla River looking eastward at the west portal of Tunnel 12, with Tunnel 11 visible beyond.* COLLECTION OF BARRIE SANFORD

FIGURE 5-6

△ FIGURE 5-7 *Tunnel 12 looking eastward towards the Coquihalla River bridge at Mile 49.6 and Tunnels 11 and 10 beyond. The open section on the left of this tunnel made it look like two tunnels, which resulted in the name Quintette Tunnels, even though only four tunnels existed. This location is now a provincial park and offers some of the most dramatic vistas in the province.* PUBLIC ARCHIVES OF CANADA.

FIGURE 5-8

FIGURE 5-9

△ FIGURE 5-8 *This unusual view was taken from the interior of Tunnel 10 looking westward. The tangent alignment of the tunnels allows Tunnels 11, 12 and 13 to also be seen. Track was laid through the Quintette Tunnels from Hope in July 1915.* COLLECTION OF BARRIE SANFORD

Quintette Tunnels

MILE	FEATURE
48.9	OTHELLO: Passing Track
49.5	Tunnel 10: 556 feet long
49.55	Tunnel 11: 100 feet long
49.6	Coquihalla River Bridge
	One half deck plate girder span: 75 feet long
49.65	Tunnel 12: 405 feet long (daylighted on north side)
49.7	Coquihalla River Bridge
	One deck truss span: 174 feet long
49.8	Tunnel 13: 246 feet long [8]

△ FIGURE 5-9 *A section of cleared right-of-way ready for grading.* COLLECTION OF BARRIE SANFORD

FIGURE 5-10

◁ FIGURE 5-10 *The tent on the left in this photo was the engineering headquarters at Coquihalla during the winter of 1913-14. Survey work continued in all but the very worst weather. Among their many duties the railway engineers maintained snow records to assist in the development of snowsheds to protect the railway from avalanches. Annual snowfalls exceeding 50 feet were common in Coquihalla Pass.* COLLECTION OF BARRIE SANFORD

FIGURE 5-11

△ FIGURE 5-11 *Completed grade ready for tracklaying. Not many sections of the line were this straight. The Coquihalla Subdivision had 234 curves aggregating 31.5 miles, the equivalent of 22 complete circles.* COLLECTION OF BARRIE SANFORD

FIGURE 5-12

FIGURE 5-13

Fraser River
Bridge
Nov. 15, '14.

△ FIGURE 5-12 *The Fraser River bridge at Hope under construction, viewed from the south bank. One pier has been completed and a pile trestle extends to the caisson where excavation for the next pier is underway. The bridge was built to allow the KVR to connect with the CPR mainline on the north side of the river.* COLLECTION OF BARRIE SANFORD

△ FIGURE 5-13 *Steelwork on the bridge superstructure being placed from the north shore in November 1914. The bridge consisted of four main through-truss spans, each 238 feet long. In terms of steel utilization it was the largest bridge on the Kettle Valley Railway.* COLLECTION OF BARRIE SANFORD

FIGURE 5-14

FIGURE 5-15

△ FIGURE 5-14 *A tracklevel view of the bridge from the south or east end. The bridge was built with an upper deck (which can be seen here) for road vehicles. The bridge still serves highway traffic, long after tracks on the lower deck have been removed.* PHOTO BY BARRIE SANFORD

◁ FIGURE 5-15 *Another large steel bridge built as part of the original Coquihalla line construction was the through arch span across Slide Creek — now more commonly called Needle Creek — at Mile 25.8 (Coquihalla Subdivision). The main span on this bridge was 320 feet long, making it the longest clear span on the Kettle Valley Railway.* COURTESY VINTAGE VISUALS (KVR102)

FIGURES 5-16 & 5-17 *Ladner Creek bridge, at Mile 36.8 (Coquihalla Subdivision) was fabricated and erected by the Canadian Bridge Company, and consisted of nine steel deck plate girder spans on steel towers, totalling 560 feet in length. Although the height of the bridge was significantly less than that of the Kettle Valley Railway's highest bridge — Trout Creek — it was still high enough to be knee-rattling to anyone but the most courageous, as* FIGURE 5-16 *of the falsework trestle used during steel placement shows.* FIGURE 5-17 *is an alternate view of the bridge, taken from the tunnel at the east end. The bridge did rate the KVR record books by being the sharpest curve of the 234 curves on the Coquihalla Subdivision — 12° 36'.*

◁ FIGURE 5-18 *This rock retaining wall at Mile 32.7 (Coquihalla Subdivision) was one of many on the KVR constructed by skilled stone masons who intricately fitted the stones together without the use of mortar. The absence of mortar made the walls free-draining, allowing water to seep between the stones rather than build up pressure which could overturn the wall. A newer extension of reinforced concrete has been built to the east of the original wall.* PHOTO BY BARRIE SANFORD

FIGURE 5-18

▽ FIGURE 5-19 *This spectacular timber frame trestle and deck truss bridge crossed Bridalveil Falls Creek — now named Fallslake Creek — at Mile 21.2 between Coquihalla and Romeo. This picture dramatically shows the great beauty and ruggedness of the canyon carved by the Coquihalla River.* PHOTO BY BARRIE SANFORD

FIGURE 5-19

FIGURE 5-20 PHOTO BY BILL PRESLEY

FIGURE 5-21 PHOTO BY BILL PRESLEY

FIGURE 5-22 COLLECTION OF BARRIE SANFORD

FIGURE 5-23
COLLECTION OF
BARRIE SANFORD

Miles from Brookmere	Telegraph and Telephone Offices	COQUIHALLA SUBDIVISION STATIONS	Telegraph Calls	Car Capacity Passing Tracks
.0	D N	BROOKMERE .... ZK B R		
		4.0		
4.0	Z	BRODIE .... ZYR		12
		Jct. Merritt S. D.		
		5.8		
9.8	Z	JULIET .... ZW		35
		8.2		
18.0	Z	COQUIHALLA ... ZYW		48
		5.5		
23.5	★	.... W		
		0.6		
24.1		ROMEO		39
		5.5		
29.6	Z	IAGO .... CW		50
		4.8		
34.4		PORTIA .... Y		46
		3.9		
38.3	★	AURUM		
		1.5		
39.8	Z	JESSICA .... W		46
		5.4		
45.2		LEAR		49
		3.7		
48.9		OTHELLO		50
		4.7		
53.6	★	C. N. R. CROSSING		
		0.7		
54.3	D Z	HOPE .... ZY K V		47
		2.3		
56.6	N Z ★	ODLUM .... R J		
		★ No Passing Track		

FIGURES 5-20 - 5-23 *As well as being an engineering marvel the Coquihalla line was something of a cultural curiosity owing to the names of the stations along the line, which were named after characters from the plays of Shakespeare. There are many colourful but incorrect stories concerning the naming of these stations. In fact, the selection was made by Andrew McCulloch, who was a great lover of the Bard's works. Several former construction workers related to the author that their fondest memory of the KVR construction days was sitting around the evening campfire listening to Andrew McCulloch recite Shakespearian poetry, invariably without reference to written text or notes. For many of these immigrant workers it was their first introduction to the power and majesty of the English language.*

Two of the Shakespearian stations had post offices. Lear had a post office from 1924 until 1932. Jessica's post office lasted from 1918 until 1942.

FIGURE 5-24

◁ FIGURE 5-24 *This newspaper ad appeared in many British Columbia papers in late July 1916 to announce the inauguration of direct passenger service between Vancouver and Nelson via Coquihalla Pass. The opening of the line heralded the achievement of the Coast-to-Kootenay rail connections which had first been suggested 29 years earlier when silver was discovered at Nelson. However, by 1916 the events of the First World War dominated the news. In many papers in the province this ad was the only coverage given the opening of the long-sought railway. Brodie station, at the junction of the Coquihalla and Merritt Subdivisions, was named after the H.W. Brodie whose name appears in the ad.*

▽ FIGURE 5-25 *Although Canadian Pacific photographer Nicholas Morant took this fine photograph of Coquihalla Pass in the early 1950s, the scene is not dramatically different from when the railway line through the pass was completed in 1916. The view is looking westward from alongside the trestle at Mile 21.7. In the distance can be seen the tunnel at Mile 23.1. The area had been devastated by a forest fire in July 1938 and at the time of this picture had not yet regrown.* COURTESY CANADIAN PACIFIC CORPORATE ARCHIVES (M5707)

FIGURE 5-25

he Independent Years

The Kettle Valley Railway: 1916-1930

THE OPENING OF THE COQUIHALLA LINE IN JULY 1916
MARKED THE TRANSITION OF THE KETTLE VALLEY RAIL-
way from what had been largely a construction organization to an
operating railway. The transition was not easy. The railway had been
committed during a period of great growth and optimism. Now, with the First World
War raging, conditions were harshly different. There were shortages of manpower and
equipment to run the railway. Costs were inflating. Much of the expected Kootenay
mining traffic went eastward to feed the war industries in central Canada, not westward over the new railway. Immigration had halted. The tourists also stayed home.
The scenic wonders of the railway held little appeal during a time of such great economic and emotional stress.

The KVR was fortunate to have Andrew McCulloch remain with the railway
management. For the next 17 years he continued to be associated with the railway,
for much of that time as general superintendent. But even McCulloch could not tame
the rebellious Coquihalla. During the first winter the line was frequently blocked by
snow or rockslides, forcing trains to be diverted via Spences Bridge and the CPR mainline. The following winter the Coquihalla line was closed all season. The link between
coast and Kootenay had shown that it would be as difficult to maintain as it had been
to achieve.

During the war, passenger train service on the KVR was cut to three days per
week. Daily service was restored on June 1, 1919 with the introduction of the "Kootenay Express" and the "Kettle Valley Express," numbered Train 11 and Train 12 respectively. These trains were to keep those designations throughout most the the KVR's
history. Until the KVR was finally absorbed by the CPR in 1931, CPR crews handled
passenger trains between Vancouver and Hope, then again east of Midway. The trains
offered coach and sleeping car accommodations, plus meal services. Meal services
were provided by a cafe-observation car or dining car, the specific offering varying
from time to time depending upon the schedule in effect. Because of the steep grades
the railway often did not carry a meal service car on the night portions of the run.
On the line between Brodie and Spences Bridge, designated the Merritt Subdivision
by the KVR, a mixed train operated daily except Sunday.

Initially the only locomotives used on the KVR were leased CPR 2-8-0's in the

◁ FIGURE 6-1
*Engine 3269 with
an eastbound passenger
train pauses in the
middle of the 182-foot-
high wooden trestle over
West Fork Canyon Creek
at Mile 87.9 (Carmi
Subdivision) on its way
from Penticton to Nelson
shortly after through-
passenger service began
in July 1916.* COLLECTION
OF BARRIE SANFORD

▽ FIGURE 6-2 *A west-bound passenger train on the same trestle as in the previous photo. The picture was probably taken between 1916 and 1919, during which time the westbound passenger train left Nelson in the morning. After the inauguration of the "Kootenay Express" and "Kettle Valley Express" in 1919 the westbound train departed Nelson in the evening, which generally put the train through Myra Canyon too early in the morning for photography. The new trains received the "express" designation because they made only selected stops on the CPR mainline through the Fraser Valley. Operating conditions on the Kettle Valley Railway made them far from fast by eastern railway standards; the 514 miles between Vancouver and Nelson were covered at an average speed of only 19.4 miles per hour. However, this was an enormous improvement in travel time compared with the days prior to the railway's opening.*
PENTICTON MUSEUM (37-2565)

3200 series, some 20 being assigned to the KVR. In the early 1920s a number of CPR 500 series D-9 4-6-0's were allocated to the railway for use on passenger and lighter freight trains. At Penticton the 2.2% grade for 27 miles east to Chute Lake and 25 miles west to Kirton required assignment of a number of locomotives to "helper" service. The 36 miles of similar grade between Hope and Coquihalla also required "helper" locomotives. On the short 2.2% grade east from Princeton to Jura, it was common for freight trains to "double" this section of grade by taking the train up to Jura in two sections. On the remainder of the line freight trains could generally run without assisting locomotives.

The steep grades and treacherous mountain conditions made work difficult for train crews. A fireman on a "helper" locomotive based at Penticton could make as many as three trips to Kirton or Chute Lake and back in a shift, during which time he might shovel 25 tons of coal. Danger was also ever present on the Kettle Valley Railway, and over the years numerous KVR employees were killed or seriously injured, principally from rockslides along the railway. However, they gave to the Kettle Valley Railway a flawless passenger record. In the 49 years which passenger trains operated on "The KV" no passenger was ever killed, and very few passengers were injured. This record was achieved despite the report of a later CPR president: "Much greater hazard is involved in keeping that route open than any other in our experience." [9]

During its first years, through-freight traffic proved disappointing for the Kettle Valley Railway. The drastic drop in copper and other metal prices after the war forced the closure of all the Boundary District mines and smelters, and cut Kootenay mining traffic as well. Fortunately, the KVR enjoyed good local traffic from lumber, coal and fruit. There were sawmills at Canford, Merritt, Brookmere, Princeton and Penticton, plus a few smaller locations, and the Nicola Pine Mills had a large logging railway operation, on the west side of the Coldwater Valley above Merritt, which provided a substantial log traffic over the railway. Coal mines at Merritt, Coalmont and Princeton provided additional traffic, as did the seasonal movement of fruit and cattle.

During the 1920s the KVR opened two branch lines. One line was committed shortly after the war ended when British Columbia Premier John Oliver announced a major land development plan for the South Okanagan as a means of accommodating returning soldiers. The KVR agreed to build a supporting branch line from Penticton

FIGURE 6-2

HYDRAULIC CREEK
BRIDGE, K.V.R.

south 36 miles to Osoyoos, although because of the staged nature of the development it was agreed that the KVR need initially build only from Okanagan Falls south to Haynes, just south of the new community of Oliver, named after the premier. A barge service on Skaha Lake would connect Okanagan Falls with a spur south from the Penticton yard until conditions justified a line along the west shore of Skaha Lake and completion of the line from Haynes to Osoyoos. The initial segment of the line opened in March 1923.

The second branch line was to Copper Mountain, south of Princeton. Construction of this line had actually started during the First World War because of the wartime demand for copper, and the line was completed in October 1920. However, it operated little more than a month before the mine was closed because of depressed copper prices. The mine and railway lay idle until August 1925 when both were reopened. For the next five years the mine provided the railway with substantial business.

Problems with the line through Coquihalla Pass proved to be the norm rather than the exception. For five of the first seven years the Coquihalla line was closed through most of the winter season, and in the early 1920s abandonment of the line was suggested. Because of the difficulty in keeping the line open the KVR in 1922 committed a major upgrading program for the line between Merritt and Spences Bridge — the original Nicola Branch — so that trains could be diverted via Merritt, perhaps permanently. Between 1922 and 1924 all major wooden bridges on the Merritt line were replaced with steel structures and heavier rails were laid. Later in the decade many of the trestles on the remaining sections of the KVR were filled in or replaced.

The investment was not wasted. On January 28, 1929 a major accident occurred on the CPR mainline between Revelstoke and Golden, when a portion of the Surprise Creek bridge collapsed. The disruption forced mainline trains to be detoured over the KVR for the next three weeks. The incident made CPR management realize the value of its southern British Columbia line as a bypass route, and soon after the mainline had been reopened the CPR announced a major work program for the KVR and the rest of the line across the province. Commitments were made to replace all remaining wooden trestles on the KVR with permanent steel structures or fills, and to introduce new and more powerful locomotives.

The CPR also stated that the operations of the Kettle Valley Railway would be taken over and integrated with the rest of the CPR system as of December 31, 1930. Legally the Kettle Valley Railway would remain owner of the trackage until 1956, when the CPR abolished its corporate subsidiary and absorbed its assets. However, the KVR's years of independence were effectively over. No longer was it the Kettle Valley Railway. It would now be the CPR's Kettle Valley Division. To train crews who had grown to love this problem railroad, it was still simply ''The KV.''

△ FIGURE 6-3 *The rugged conditions of southern British Columbia gave the Kettle Valley Railway plenty of problems from the day it commenced operations. On April 30, 1918 a log jam piled up against the main pier of the Kettle River bridge at Mile 15.5 (Carmi Subdivision), causing the restricted river to undermine the east abutment of the bridge. In this picture fresh piles have been driven to allow train service to resume using the bridge.* COLLECTION OF BARRIE SANFORD

△ FIGURE 6-4 *Crews contemplate a washout about a mile west of Coquihalla. The Coquihalla River at th point seems hardly more than a creek.* COLLECTION OF BARRIE SANFORD

FIGURE 6-5
COURTESY ANDREW
McCULLOCH FOUNDATION

☐ FIGURES 6-5 & 6-6 *The early years of Kettle Valley Railway operation were not all problems. In September 1919 the KVR hosted a highly successful royal tour for Prince Edward, the Prince of Wales. On the morning of September 29 a special train with the royal party ran from Vancouver to Hope, where the train was broken into two sections for the trip over the KVR to Penticton. The train order shown in FIGURE 6-5 was issued to instruct a meet between Train 11 and the two sections of the royal train at Portia. A lithographed publication titled "Over the Kettle Valley Route" was issued specifically for the royal party. The cover of one of the few remaining copies is shown in FIGURE 6-6.*

FIGURE 6-6 COLLECTION OF BARRIE SANFORD

KETTLE VALLEY RAILWAY COMPANY

FORM 31

FORM 31

TRAIN ORDER NO. 33   Sept. 29th.1919.   19

To Eng 3280   AT   Hope B.C.   M.
Royal Psgr Extra 3260

                              OPR.:
X

No 11 engine 3205 meet psgr extra 3280 East and Royal
Psgr Extra 3260 East at Portia.

C.R.A.

Conductor and Engineer must each have a copy of this order.

REPEATED AT   15:14   M.

CONDUCTOR	ENGINEER	TRAIN	MADE	TIME	OPERATOR

OVER THE KETTLE VALLEY ROUTE BRITISH COLUMBIA

FIGURE 6-7

Miles from Princeton	Telegraph and Telephone Offices	COPPER MOUNTAIN SUBDIVISION STATIONS	Telegraph Calls	Car Capacity Passing Tracks
13.6		END OF TRACK		
		0.3		
13.3		COPPER MOUNTAIN		5
		7.7		
5.6	D	ALLENBY......W B Y		11
		5.6		
.0	D N Z	PRINCETON..YWCB O D		

FIGURE 6-8

▲ FIGURES 6-7 & 6-8 *After the opening of its mainline the KVR undertook construction of two branch lines. The first line was from Princeton south to Copper Mountain, where the wartime demand for copper resulted in the opening of a large copper mine. Twenty-four trestles and four tunnels were required. FIGURE 6-8 shows construction underway, with the partly excavated tunnel at Mile 11.3 in the distance.* COLLECTION OF BARRIE SANFORD

FIGURE 6-9

Miles from Penticton	Telegraph and Telephone Offices	OSOYOOS SUBDIVISION STATIONS	Telegraph Calls	Car Capacity Passing Tracks
36.4		END OF TRACK		
		0.3		
36.1	D	OSOYOOS......CYR S O		23
		5.8		
30.3		ELLIS		11
		4.2		
26.1	★	HAYNES......Y		
		3.4		
22.7	D	OLIVER......W J O		24
		5.8		
16.9		McINTYRE		19
		6.3		
10.6		OKANAGAN FALLS		10
		3.7		
6.9	Z	KALEDEN		33
		4.8		
2.1		SKAHA		14
		2.1		
.0	D N	PENTICTON......YK S		
★ No Passing Track				

▲ FIGURE 6-9 *The second KVR branch line was the Osoyoos Subdivision, although it did not actually reach Osoyoos until 1944. As of 1923 the line ran only between Penticton and the north end of Skaha Lake, and between Okanagan Falls and Haynes, with connections by barge service on Skaha Lake. While the new settlers along the line awaited maturation of the fruit trees they had planted, cantaloupe were grown between the rows of developing trees. As a consequence the train on the line was dubbed the "Cantaloupe Express."* COLLECTION OF BARRIE SANFORD

▽ FIGURE 6-10 *As well as train operation the Kettle Valley Railway provided a telegraph service. This telegram announcing the death of Thomas Shaughnessy in 1923 was saved by Andrew McCulloch, to whom it was sent. The writings of McCulloch show that he had great regard for Shaughnessy, and was highly flattered by the CPR president's choice of him to engineer the Kettle Valley Railway. McCulloch was aware that the decision to commit construction of the KVR was primarily Shaughnessy's. There was little other support for the undertaking in CPR management, and quite likely the Kettle Valley Railway would not have been built had it not been for the personal conviction of Shaughnessy that coast and Kootenay must be connected by rail. Coleman, who himself later became CPR president, made an additional comment about Shaughnessy: "He never regarded the C.P.R. as a mere business enterprise, but was determined that in all its activities it would contribute to Canada's development and reputation."[10]* COURTESY ANDREW McCULLOCH FOUNDATION

FIGURE 6-10

KETTLE VALLEY RAILWAY COMPANY

FORM 8

FIRST SAFETY LAST ALWAYS

TELEGRAM

This form to be used for Railway Service messages.

Time Filed..................M.

The exact sending and receiving time, initials of sending operator, and signal of office with which business is done, must be plainly noted on face of message.

FIRST SAFETY LAST ALWAYS

Winnipeg Man Dec 10 th - 23
via Merritt

A McCulloch Brookmere

Regret to advise you that our chairman Lord Shaughnessy passed away this evening   Please have Flags placed at half Mast until after the funeral

2040K   D C Coleman

▽ FIGURE 6-12 *A view of the interior of Penticton roundhouse. The roundhouse was originally built with four stalls, but two more stalls were later added. Penticton was the headquarters for Kettle Valley Railway operations and the base for most of the approximately 20 locomotives which were assigned to the KVR in the early 1920s.* PENTICTON MUSEUM – STOCKS FAMILY COLLECTION

FIGURE 6-12

◁ FIGURE 6-11 *Penticton roundhouse employees pose on Engine 3454 about 1922.* PENTICTON MUSEUM

1. Eddie Aldridge
2. Bob Brown
3. Leonard Gardiner
4. Joe Collett
5. Jeff MacDonald
6. Ed McDonald
7. Art Cosser
8. Bill Monks
9. Bill Johnson
10. Ed Joyce
11. George Whaton
12. John Baptist
13. Fred Bean
14. Fred Bradburn
15. Dick Whitehead
16. Charles Lye
17. Bill Boyce
18. Jim Clary
19. Shorty Aldridge
20. Archie Simpson
21. Unknown
22. Ernie Mitchell
23. Bill Brown
24. Alf Atherton
25. Alec Crawford
26. George Barr
27. Ham Swift
28. Horace Reeves
29. Clarence Finnis
30. George Smyth
31. Fred Milligan
32. Bob Roberts

FIGURE 6-13

△ FIGURE 6-13 *CPR D9 class 4-6-0 locomotive 572 poses in front of Penticton station with a passenger train in the early 1920s. Locomotives of the D9 class were surprisingly powerful despite their relatively small size, which made them well suited for the KVR. Note the horse-drawn wagon transferring express. Posing with 572 are J.G. "Tommy" McLellan, Bert McLellan and Ed Sprague.* PENTICTON MUSEUM – STOCKS FAMILY COLLECTION

▽ FIGURE 6-14 *A D9 also appears to be commanding this westbound passenger train at Brodie, the junction point of the Merritt Subdivision with the Coquihalla Subdivision. The passenger train is crossing the Coldwater River bridge at Mile 4.1 (Coquihalla Subdivision), while an eastbound engine is waiting in the clear on the Merritt Subdivision. Several work cars stand on the third leg of the wye track forming the junction. The fresh earth on the embankment suggests that the original trestle approaching the bridge has just been filled. The wooden Howe Truss bridge the train is crossing was replaced by a steel deck bridge in 1929.* COLLECTION OF BARRIE SANFORD

FIGURE 6-14

FIGURE 6-16

△ FIGURE 6-15 *The job of railroading was enjoyable to many who lived it, but it was a career path that was seldom easy and often dangerous. Locomotive 3478 sits in Brookmere yard after hitting a rockslide and overturning just west of Brodie on March 28, 1930 killing fireman Bob Barwick.* COLLECTION OF BARRIE SANFORD

▢ FIGURE 6-16 *In this picture taken on board a westbound freight near Juliet the "stemwinder," brakewheels of the freight cars are clearly visible. These brakewheels could only be turned from atop the cars, and as the special instruction in Figure 6-17 states, trainmen were required to ride atop the freight cars while descending grades of 2.0% or greater. Such a task was uncomfortable and risky, especially in fierce winter conditions. Numerous brakemen lost their lives when a train lurched or stopped unexpectedly. One fell from a train — luckily without serious injury — when an elephant on a circus train reached up with its trunk from inside the car and pulled the brakeman from his perch by the brakewheel.* COLLECTION OF BILL PRESLEY

Trainmen's Position when Descending Grades. 8. On all freight trains when descending grades of two per cent (2%) or over, front and rear trainmen must have clubs in their possession and be out on top of train, the conductor to ride in cupola to observe air pressure and to see that trainmen are in their proper places. If conductor considers engineer is not exercising proper judgment, he must stop train by use of conductor's valve in accordance with Air Brake Rule No. 6.

FIGURE 6-17

▽ FIGURE 6-18 *Lumber traffic was an important component of the KVR's freight business. This picture shows an early sawmill at Chute Lake, viewed looking eastward along the rail line. Several boxcars are positioned at the mill for loading. The water tower is of standard CPR design, built with octagonal outer shell and interior stove to keep the water in the tank from freezing during winter conditions. Judging by the position of the float on top of the tower a freight train has likely just crested the grade from Penticton. A through freight engine and one or more helper locomotives could easily take on 5000 gallons of water each after the climb from Penticton.* COLLECTION OF MRS. J.H. PERCIVAL

FIGURE 6-18

FIGURE 6-19

▷ FIGURE 6-19 *During the KVR's years of independent operation prior to 1931 Hope was a significant point on the railway. This was the KVR's western terminus where trains would be turned over to CPR crews for operation through to Vancouver and also a base for helper engines assisting trains up Coquihalla Pass. As a consequence the KVR in 1917 built this three stall enginehouse at Hope. When KVR operations were absorbed by the CPR in 1931 train crews worked straight through between Vancouver and Brookmere, and helper engines came from Ruby Creek or Brookmere. That resulted in the closure of Hope as a terminus.* VANCOUVER PUBLIC LIBRARY (56175)

FIGURE 6-20

◁ FIGURE 6-20 *Hope was also significant as a loading point for automobiles being transported across the Hope Mountains to Princeton. The service was heavily used until 1926, when the road through the Fraser Canyon was opened, allowing automobile drivers to route to Princeton via Spences Bridge. The Hope-Princeton Highway was not completed until 1949.* COURTESY VINTAGE VISUALS (KVR 099)

FIGURE 6-21

◁ FIGURE 6-21 *Hope, looking eastward along the railway towards Coquihalla Pass in the early 1920s. A flatcar loaded with autos waits on the siding for the next eastbound freight. The passenger car beside it is likely a dining car set out from an eastbound train to save hauling it up the Coquihalla grade. It will be picked up by a westbound train. An interesting comparison picture is Figure 9-1.* VANCOUVER PUBLIC LIBRARY (56089)

△ FIGURE 6-22 *Engine 3512 and unidentified crew with an empty ore train at Allenby ready to return to Copper Mountain. Allenby was the site of the concentrator mill for ore from the Granby mine at Copper Mountain. The KVR assigned a 15-car ore train to the run which would generally make three round trips per day between the mine and mill. The mine ran from 1925 until 1930, and from 1937 until 1957. In 1927, an average year, the KVR handled 13,696 cars of ore and 861 cars of concentrates on its Copper Mountain Subdivision.* COURTESY VINTAGE VISUALS (CPR 094)

▽ FIGURE 6-23 *Electrical power for the Copper Mountain mine and Allenby concentrator mill was provided by its coal-fired thermal power plant at Princeton, built by Granby and officially opened August 1, 1925. Coal for the plant initially came from a nearby mine, but later came by rail from Coalmont Collieries and other mines. The plant remained for a considerable time after the closure of Copper Mountain and was not demolished until 1968.* PROVINCIAL ARCHIVES OF BRITISH COLUMBIA (CAT. HP453-88; NEG. F4132)

FIGURES 6-24 & 6-25 *These two photographs are of the Coalmont Collieries powerplant and railcar loading plant at Coalmont. The company's mine was located at Blakeburn, several miles up the hillside behind the mine, and coal was delivered to the loading plant by the aerial tramway visible in the pictures. Coal from the Blakeburn mine was generally regarded as among the best steam coal in western North America. As a consequence the CPR, KVR, GN and even Canadian National were all customers of Coalmont Collieries. The KVR used only Coalmont coal for its locomotives until the CPR takeover in 1931, after which Merritt coal was substituted as an economy measure. The mine suffered a major explosion on August 13, 1930 which killed 45 men. Thereafter production declined steadily until the final closure of the mine on April 8, 1940. One of the mine houses in the picture on the right survives as a private residence.* COURTESY VINTAGE VISUALS (KVR 162).

FIGURE 6-25

FIGURE 6-26 COURTESY VINTAGE VISUALS (GNR 017)

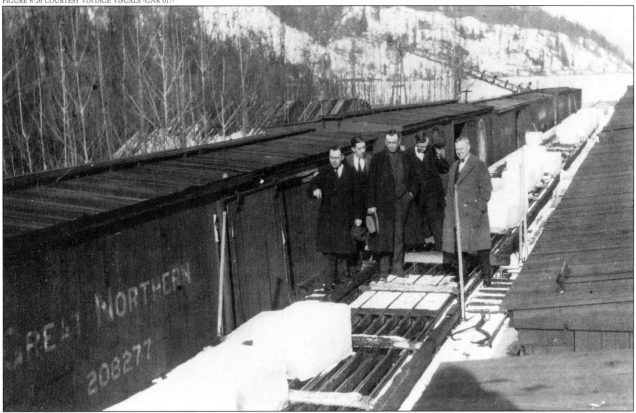

FIGURES 6-26 & 6-27 *In the age before mechanical refrigeration vast amounts of ice had to be "harvested" from the lakes at higher elevations during winter and stored in sawdust insulated icehouses at the major terminals for use in packing reefer cars carrying fruit during summer. Ice also had to be cut for cooling passenger cars. The KVR had a large icehouse at Penticton and generally cut its ice from Osprey Lake. The Great Northern cut ice for almost all of its Washington State icehouses from Otter Lake near Tulameen, where these two photographs were taken. Blocks of ice would be cut by hand, then dragged by horse to a boxcar loader which would move the ice between rows of waiting cars. The size of the operation was nothing short of incredible. In 1919 — the record year — 3000 cars of ice were loaded and shipped in only 15 days. The advent of mechanical ice production in the early 1920s resulted in a rapid decline in the need for natural ice.*

FIGURE 6-27 COURTESY VINTAGE VISUALS (GNR 018)

FIGURES 6-28, 6-29, 6-30 *The close proximity of Coquihalla Pass to the Pacific coast weather systems and its rapid rise made snow conditions on the Coquihalla Subdivision more difficult than anywhere on the Canadian Pacific Railway system. To combat snow the Kettle Valley Railway used snowsheds, rotary plows, wing plows and large gangs of men with shovels. Figure 6-28 shows rotary plow 400805 at Hope in August 1929 as the plow awaited another winter. Rotary plows were not particularly successful on the Coquihalla line, principally because snowslides often contained rocks and trees which destroy the cutting blades. When bulldozers became available they became a key snowfighting tool and the CPR eliminated all but five of the original 15 snowsheds on the Coquihalla Subdivision. FIGURES 6-29 and 6-30 show rotary plows in action.*

FIGURE 6-31

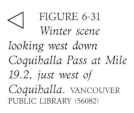 FIGURE 6-31
Winter scene looking west down Coquihalla Pass at Mile 19.2, just west of Coquihalla. VANCOUVER PUBLIC LIBRARY (56082)

FIGURE 6-32

FIGURE 6-32
Westbound wingplow at Cultus Creek trestle, Mile 22.7, just west of Tunnel 4. VANCOUVER PUBLIC LIBRARY (56087)

FIGURE 6-33

FIGURE 6-33
A view looking westward towards the east switch of Romeo passing track. A plow train is passing through Shed 2 in the distance. COLLECTION OF BARRIE SANFORD

Kettle Valley Railway Dateline

1916 - 1930

1916-06-22   CPR Engine 522 with eastbound silk train collided with Engine 3100 at Merritt. This was the first mainline train diverted over the KVR and only silk train ever diverted.

1917-01-30   Original Brookmere station destroyed by fire.

1917-07-18   Special train operated to Brodie to dedicate name after General Passenger Agent of the CPR.

1917-08-03   GN private car with Ralph Budd and other GN officials ran from Hope to Princeton on tail of KVR freight train.

1917-12-13   Rockslide knocked caboose of plow train 700 feet into canyon between Coquihalla and Romeo. One killed.

1918-03-16   Passenger train service between Penticton and Nelson cut to three days per week.

1918-03-20   Contract awarded to W.P. Tierney for construction of Copper Mountain line.

1918-04-29   Passenger train service between Penticton and Vancouver cut to three days per week.

1918-04-30   Log jam knocked out bridge over Kettle River at Mile 15.5 (Carmi Subdivision).

1919-05-27   Nicola Pine Mills sawmill at Canford and 13 cars of lumber destroyed by fire. Replacement mill later built at Merritt.

1919-06-01   Daily passenger train service between Vancouver and Nelson resumed. Train 11 and Train 12 introduced.

1919-09-29   Prince of Wales special train ran from Vancouver to Penticton. Left Penticton for Midway late the next day.

1920-03-03   KVR and British Columbia government signed agreement for joint development of South Okanagan Valley.

1920-03-30   Construction of Nicola Pine Mills logging railway at Pine started.

1920-05-16   GN ran special train from Oroville to Coalmont with President Ralph Budd and other officials for a tour of Coalmont Collieries.

1920-07-08   KVR announced contract for construction of 2.5 miles of line from Penticton yard to Skaha Lake awarded to P.J. Salvus.

1920-07-20   Six freight cars derailed at Thalia after running loose downgrade from Brookmere.

1920-10-07   Copper Mountain line completed. Mine closed in December and remained closed until August 1925.

1920-12-21   Princeton Coal & Land Company tipple and four cars of coal destroyed by fire.

1920-12-27   Mixed train service on Merritt Subdivision reduced from daily except Sunday to three times per week.

1921-12-01   KVR took over operation of Princeton station from GN.

1922-03-22   Wing plow derailed and fell 250 feet into canyon at Mile 20.8 (Coquihalla Subdivision). One injured.

1922-07-31   Tracklaying started at Okanagan Falls.

1922-12-10   Engine 3268 and several cars of westbound freight derailed at Mile 103.5 (Carmi Subdivision).

1923-03-20   Railway Commission approved line from Penticton yard to Skaha Lake and from Okanagan Falls to just south of Haynes for operation.

1924-05-24   Special excursion train operated from Penticton to Oliver and return for Victoria Day.

1924-11-26   Engine 3206 and several passenger cars of Train 11 derailed at Mile 40.0 (Carmi Subdivision). One killed.

1924-12-24   Engine 3267 ran loose on CPR mainline eastward from Spences Bridge, nearly causing collision with westbound passenger train.

1925-01-20   Last recorded GN ice train left Tulameen.

1925-02-23   Engine 580 and several passenger cars of Train 12 derailed at Mile 73.8 (Princeton Subdivision). Private car "British Columbia" overturned.

1925-04-12   Engine 3217 on eastbound freight ran into rockslide at Mile 60.5 (Carmi Subdivision). Line blocked until April 18.

Dateline cont'd

1925-05-26	Circus train of 29 cars moved from Hope to Penticton.
1925-08-22	Baby born on board Train 12 just west of Princeton.
1925-08-24	Allenby concentrator reopened.
1926-01-02	Nicola station closed.
1926-03-22	Engine 3401 and two cars of westbound freight fell through damaged bridge at Mile 28.3 (Coquihalla Subdivision) and slid down into canyon. No injuries.
1926-08-28	Jail escapee stole locomotive from Merritt yard and ran it nearly to Nicola before being recaptured.
1926-09-05	Engine 3401 and 25 freight cars derailed at Mile 40.5 (Coquihalla Subdivision) following runaway downgrade from Iago. Four crew killed and unknown number of hobos may also have been killed.
1927-09-13	Two special passenger trains of 13 cars each operated from Hope to Princeton and Allenby with delegates to a mining convention.
1929-03-17	Special passenger train ran from Princeton to Copper Mountain to dedicate cairn in memory of nine men killed at Copper Mountain 1928-03-18.
1930-03-28	Engine 3478 on westbound freight hit rockslide at Mile 4.4 (Coquihalla Subdivision). One killed.
1930-07-10	First car interchanged between CN barge spur line and KVR at Penticton.
1930-11-15	Copper Mountain mine closed.
1930-12-10	Contract for construction of line along west side of Skaha Lake awarded.

▽ FIGURE 6-34 *The collapse of the Surprise Creek bridge on the CPR mainline in January 1929 resulted in the longest sustained diversion of mainline trains over the KVR in history. For nearly three weeks most CPR traffic used the KVR, resulting in the assignment of some 30 extra crews and dozens of locomotives to the KVR. In this interesting picture a diverted mainline passenger train heads west across Trout Creek bridge at West Summerland under the power of three locomotives.* COURTESY VINTAGE VISUALS (KVR 018)

FIGURE 6-34

ard Times

The Kettle Valley Railway: 1931-1945

THE TAKEOVER OF THE KETTLE VALLEY RAILWAY BY THE CPR AT THE START OF 1931 GAVE CANADIAN PACIFIC A truly integrated rail network in British Columbia. However, the unification had the misfortune of being coincident with the early stages of a long period of economic depression in Canada, and the detrimental effects of the depression more than offset any gains made by the amalgamation. Late in 1930 the Copper Mountain mine closed, slicing off a quarter of the KVR's freight tonnage. The Trail smelter, the KVR's other most significant traffic generator, greatly curtailed production. The summer of 1931 was the hottest and driest in southern British Columbia since records started being kept before the turn of the century, destroying the Okanagan fruit crop that year. Grasshoppers by the millions swept the countryside. Their broken carcasses so greased the rails that trains could sometimes hardly move. Forest fires ravaged the southern interior. In all it was a discouraging year for the new Kettle Valley Division.

Despite the many difficulties, the CPR authorized construction of an eight-mile-long line along the west shore of Skaha Lake linking Penticton with Okanagan Falls, thereby eliminating barge service on Skaha Lake. Construction was carried out in 1931 and the line opened in October of that year. The CPR also continued its bridge replacement program begun in 1929. Large steel bridges were built to replace the two largest wooden trestles in Myra Canyon and at Dry Creek, Mile 50.4, on the Princeton Subdivision. Trestles which were not replaced with steel bridges or fills were renewed with fresh timber. Early in 1932 the company also transfered to the Kettle Valley Division a number of powerful 5100 series 2-8-2 locomotives. Considering the economic times, the moves were a bold affirmation of the CPR's faith in Canada and the long term earning potential of the KVR.

However, even as large a corporation as the Canadian Pacific Railway could not continue major capital expenditures in the face of protracted low revenues. By 1933 many of the improvement programs had been curtailed. Severe cuts in operational expenses were also made. Numerous employees were laid off. For much of the remainder of the decade the rail line through Coquihalla Pass was deliberately closed each winter as a result of CPR policy to accept the inevitable Coquihalla winters and divert trains over the longer line via Spences Bridge beginning in the late fall.

◁ FIGURE 7-1 *The years from 1931 to 1945 represented hard times for the Kettle Valley Railway. First a decade of depression starved the railway of needed traffic and revenue. Then six years of war thrust great demands upon the railway while at the same time denying it many of the resources needed to operate. The difficulties generated no sympathy from Mother Nature, who continued to obstruct the railway at whim. Here engine 5178 at the head of Train 12 stops at one of several major washouts that occurred near Erris during the 1930's while passengers prepare to hike around to another train behind the photographer.* COLLECTION OF LANCE CAMP

The depression also spelled the end for many rail lines in southern British Columbia. In 1935 the KVR abandoned its North Fork line. The Great Northern went into a major retrenchment, and the company abandoned much of the trackage which had been the focal point of its "war" with the CPR three or four decades earlier. In April 1934 GN train service between Hedley and Princeton was suspended because of flood damage to a bridge. Service was never restored, and in 1937 this section of the line was formally abandoned.

The abandonment of the GN east of Princeton orphaned the section of GN trackage between Princeton and Brookmere, which legally remained the property of its subsidiary VV&E and which was in regular use by KVR trains under rights extended by the "Tulameen Agreement" of 1914. The abandonment also left the GN with no possible way of utilizing its rights to the Coquihalla line, for which it was still obligated to continue paying the KVR approximately $150,000 per year under the terms of the "Coquihalla Agreement" signed in 1913. Indeed, the healthy payment from the GN was probably all that prevented the CPR from abandoning the Coquihalla line in the 1930s. The GN appeared reluctant to make a cash offer to cancel the agreement, all the while hoping the CPR would become fed up with the Coquihalla "headache" and abandon the line on its own, thereby effectively relieving the GN of any obligation to continue paying for rights to use the trackage.

The CPR appeared equally at odds. On one hand it is known that several prominent CPR officials favoured abandonment of the line. But abandonment of the line would end the significant annual payment from the GN, for which there was still little corporate fondness in the CPR. When it became obvious during the Second World War that the CPR would retain the line, the GN conceded the stalemate. In 1944 it paid $4.5 million to cancel the "Coquihalla Agreement." The following year it sold the Princeton-Brookmere trackage to the CPR for one-third that amount. The one train which GN operated over the Coquihalla line in September 1916 may well have been the most expensive train ride in history!

Late in 1936 the civil war in Spain boosted the price of copper, prompting reopening of the mine at Copper Mountain in June of 1937. This surge in business was a prelude to the future. In September 1939 Canada entered the Second World War, and almost overnight the depression-shrouded 1930s gave way to a new decade

▽ FIGURE 7-2
Locomotive 579 with Train 11 at Princeton in 1931. At this time Train 11 was still on the westbound schedule established in 1919 which featured a morning departure from Penticton. It would shortly be changed to an evening departure from Penticton, thus matching the overnight schedule between Vancouver and Penticton which Train 12 had always maintained.
COLLECTION OF LANCE CAMP

FIGURE 7-2

FIGURE 7-3

dominated by the industry and commerce of war. Demand for copper, lead, coal and lumber skyrocketed. Furthermore, the war came at a time when the Canadian west coast had become established as a significant industrial centre. Therefore much of the Kootenay mineral traffic came westward. Okanagan fruit production was also pushed to record limits by the demand for food in war-torn Great Britain. In the latter years of the war more than 14,000 railcars of fruit left the Okanagan annually.

Early in the war the CPR realized that this massive increase in freight traffic would force it to end its policy of relinquishing the Coquihalla line to the ravages of winter after the first few snowfalls. Coquihalla Pass proved to be far from willing to oblige the CPR in this regard. While fighting to keep open the lifeline of the west coast war industries, more than one denim-clad soldier of the KVR was required to pay a price equal to that of his khaki-clad comrade in Europe. However, the sacrifices of the Kettle Valley Railway employees were not in vain. Between 1940 and 1945 the aggregate time which the Coquihalla line was closed was less than the time lost in any single winter season of the previous decade.

The demands of the war also resulted in the completion of the Osoyoos line. In order to increase fruit shipments to Great Britain, the KVR was granted special government permission in 1944 to extend the line from the end of track just south of Oliver to Osoyoos. The significance of the permission can be gained from the fact that this was the only railway construction of consequence undertaken in all of Canada during the Second World War. Grading work for the extension began in July 1944. The entire 10 miles of line was graded in a few weeks by only 15 men using bulldozers, a sharp contrast with the thousands of labourers who had been needed for the construction of the Kettle Valley Railway mainline a generation earlier. The last spike on the line was driven at Osoyoos on December 28, 1944. With the exception of a few minor industrial spurs, this was to be the last piece of trackage constructed on the Kettle Valley Railway.

FIGURE 7-4

△ FIGURE 7-4 *Despite the effects of the Depression the CPR continued much of its upgrading of the KVR announced in early 1929, which included replacement of the two largest wooden frame trestles in Myra Canyon with steel structures. FIGURE 7-4 shows steel being placed by the Canadian Bridge Company for the new bridge over West Fork Canyon Creek during the summer of 1932 to replace the earlier wooden trestle, which is the same structure that appears in FIGURE 7-3. Note how the steel towers of the new bridge have been built up between the bents of the wooden trestle so that train service need not be seriously interrupted by construction.* PENTICTON MUSEUM

▽ FIGURE 7-5 *This photo shows a westbound passenger train on the bridge after completion of steelwork and removal of the wooden trestle. The train is comprised entirely of steel cars, introduced in 1931 to replace the earlier wooden cars as part of general upgrading.*
PENTICTON MUSEUM

FIGURE 7-5

 FIGURES 7-6 & 7-7 *Other improvements on the Kettle Valley Railway undertaken during the early years of the Depression were the introduction of P1 class 5100 series 2-8-2 locomotives and completion of trackage along the west shore of Skaha Lake. FIGURE 7-6 shows locomotive 5178 at Penticton station shortly after her assignment to Vancouver-Penticton passenger train service in early 1932. In a pose looking very much like a model railroad, in FIGURE 7-7 a diminutive Consolidation steps over the long pile trestle across the Okanagan River at the south end of Skaha Lake at Mile 10.2 (Osoyoos Subdivision) with a train of loaded fruit ''reefers'' for Penticton shortly after the line's completion in 1931. The cars will be iced at Penticton yard later that afternoon, then loaded on the barge for Kelowna that evening or sent westward. With this dispatch their cargo will likely be on market counters within 48 hours. Fruit provided the main traffic for the Osoyoos Subdivision.*

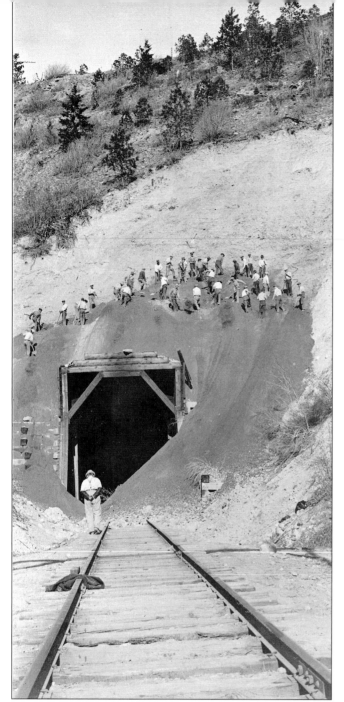

FIGURE 7-8

△ FIGURE 7-8 *On April 11, 1934 a landslide buried the west portal of the Princeton Tunnel, Mile 71.3 Princeton Subdivision. In this photo several dozen men labour — antlike — on the slope above the tunnel portal clearing away dirt which might slide down upon the tracks. The local paper that week advertised: "Work available. Bring your own shovel. 25 cents per hour."* COLLECTION OF BARRIE SANFORD

FIGURE 7-9

△ FIGURE 7-9 *Further frustrations! Engine 3640 holds a piledriver in position as piles are placed on a temporary trestle across a washout near Erris created when a beaver dam gave way and overwhelmed the culvert under the railway roadbed in 1939. The piles are 90 feet in length, making the workers in the scene appear almost insignificant.* COLLECTION OF BARRIE SANFORD

FIGURE 7-10

▷ FIGURE 7-10 *Though the Great Depression was generally a time of retrenchment for the railways, some positive innovations did take place. In 1936 the CPR unveiled the F2A class 3000 series 4-4-4 locomotives which represented the first semi-streamlined steam locomotives acquired by the company. Prior to entering service in the fall of 1936 engine 3001 made a tour of western Canada, and was on display in Penticton on September 17, 1936, as seen in FIGURE 7-10. The clean design by CPR Chief of Motive Power H.B. Bowen introduced with this engine was a forerunner of the later "Royal Hudson" class of locomotives.* COLLECTION OF BARRIE SANFORD

FIGURE 7-11

FIGURE 7-12

FIGURE 7-11 *Train 12 halted on Trout Creek bridge for this dramatic publicity photo taken in the 1930s.* PENTICTON MUSEUM — STOCKS FAMILY COLLECTION

FIGURE 7-12 *Happy engine crew: Fireman Harry Percival and engineman Bill Borthwick pose in the cab of their 2-8-0 before setting out on a run.* COLLECTION OF MRS. J.H. PERCIVAL

FIGURE 7-13

◁ FIGURE 7-13 *The presence of 2520 in this winter scene at Brookmere is an almost certain indication that the Coquihalla line was closed at the time and this 1907 built 4-6-2 has come from North Bend with a passenger train detouring via Spences Bridge.* COLLECTION OF BARRIE SANFORD

FIGURE 7-14

◁ FIGURE 7-14 *On the night of January 20-21, 1935 a record 12 feet of snow fell at Coquihalla. Here, railway crews salvage cargo from a boxcar knocked off the tracks by a snowslide at Romeo. The boxcar has been cabled to the mountainside to prevent it from falling further into the canyon.* COLLECTION OF BARRIE SANFORD

FIGURE 7-15

◁ FIGURE 7-15 *Further west more cars lie toppled by snowslides.* COLLECTION OF BARRIE SANFORD

▷ FIGURE 7-17 *In this dramatic winter scene engine 3613 is leaving Brookmere with a freight train bound for Hope. The engine is working hard, as a 1.2% grade leads back towards Princeton from the crest of the divide between the Fraser and Columbia River systems in front of the station. Brookmere was unusual in that two through tracks were built on each side of the station, unlike most stations which had unimpeded public access from one side or only a local track at the rear. Under the "Coquihalla Agreement" between the KVR and VV&E the station and water tower at Brookmere were to be shared by the two companies. The land north of the station was designated for the KVR, where it built a three-stall roundhouse, coal chute and other facilities. The VV&E never used its land on the south side, and the two "VV&E" tracks on the south side of the station came to be used for general KVR operation. The water tower also had two spouts to serve both railways.* PHOTO BY BILL PRESLEY

◁ FIGURE 7-16 *The fireman of this engine looks from the cab window as crews attempt to dig out his locomotive east of Romeo.* COLLECTION OF BARRIE SANFORD

FIGURE 7-16

FIGURE 7-18 PHOTO BY BARRIE SANFORD

FIGURE 7-19 PROVINCIAL ARCHIVES OF BRITISH COLUMBIA (CAT. HP66714; NEG. F3637)

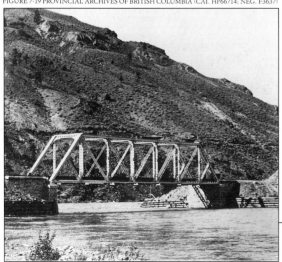

FIGURES 7-18 & 7-19 *Bridges are normally considered static structures. However, bridges occasionally have a more dynamic history. FIGURE 7-18 shows the 163-foot-long steel through-truss bridge over the Nicola River at Mile 149.4 (Princeton Subdivision) just below Canford. In 1922 the KVR committed replacement of all the wooden Howe Truss bridges on the line between Spences Bridge and Merritt, and in 1929 the truss bridge from the Nicola River crossing on the CPR mainline just east of Spences Bridge was disassembled and moved 28 miles upstream to a new crossing of the same river. Later the CPR decided to strengthen the bridge by building a second truss around the earlier one. FIGURE 7-19 shows the original bridge in its mainline position, where it had been built not long after the major flooding of 1894. Note the pins in the ends of the truss members on the lower cord. This is almost certain evidence that the original structure predates 1910.*

FIGURE 7-20

FIGURE 7-21

FIGURE 7-22

◁ FIGURE 7-20 *An interesting human portrait: Martin Grainger sets out his ''flag'' at Belfort flagstop, then naps while awaiting his train, which has been delayed five hours by a washout.*
PROVINCIAL ARCHIVES OF BRITISH COLUMBIA CAT. HP52270; (NEG. C5660)

▽ FIGURE 7-21 *Merritt station, viewed from atop the railway water tower. This picture is believed to have been taken in 1938.*
COURTESY VINTAGE VISUALS (KVR 181)

▷ FIGURE 7-22 *When the word railroader is mentioned the most common image which comes to mind is of engineers and firemen, or perhaps a uniformed passenger train conductor. But the railways were equally dependent on many other employees to keep the trains running. Perhaps least recognized were the section foremen. Section foremen lived in isolated railway buildings — appropriately called sectionhouses — and were responsible for a daily foot patrol of their "section", usually requiring about 15 miles of walking per day. Often their families would live with them in their lonely outpost. This picture shows Mrs. Millership, wife of the Arawana section foreman, proudly standing in front of her beautifully maintained lawn and garden.* COLLECTION OF JOE SMUIN

Kettle Valley Railway Dateline

1931 - 1945

1931-01-01	Kettle Valley Railway operations absorbed into CPR and became the Kettle Valley Division.
1931-01-19	Construction of line along Skaha Lake started.
1931-07-22	Tracklaying on Skaha Lake line started.
1931-08-26	Tracklaying on Skaha Lake line completed.
1932-01-23	Engine 583 running light eastbound collided with engine 566 westbound with Merritt mixed train at Mile 2.6 (Coquihalla Subdivision). One injured.
1932-02-27	Engine 579 of eastbound train taking rotary plow to Nelson derailed at Mile 4.5 (Carmi Subdivision). One injured.
1934-04-09	Major washout at Mile 55.2 (Princeton Subdivision).
1934-04-11	West end of Princeton Tunnel caved in.
1934-04-23	GN bridge over Similkameen River at Princeton damaged by floodwaters. GN never resumed train service into Princeton.
1935-01-25	Bridge over Tulameen River at Mile 75.5 (Princeton Subdivision) smashed out by ice jam. Through service not restored until 1935-02-11.
1935-09-27	Railway Commission approved abandonment of North Fork Subdivision.
1935-01-06	Last day of CPR passenger boat operation on Okanagan Lake.
1936-09-17	Streamlined train at Penticton.
1937-06-12	Copper Mountain mine reopened.
1937-11-23	Engine 3688 on westbound freight fell through bridge over Tulameen River at Mile 79.8 (Princeton Subdivision) while bridge being rebuilt. Two killed.
1938-07-21	Wooden trestles at Mile 21.5, 21.7 and 22.3 (Coquihalla Subdivision) destroyed by fire. Line closed until 1938-09-21.
1941-11-14	Engine 5178 on Train 11 derailed by slide at Mile 25.3 (Coquihalla Subdivision) and plunged into canyon. Two killed.
1941-12-15	New Penticton station opened. Passenger trains no longer routed down to wharf.
1944-06-30	CPR announced contract for construction of 10 miles of line from Haynes to Osoyoos awarded to Fred Mannix & Company and Dutton Brothers.
1944-11-25	Engine 5101 on Train 12 blew its boiler at Mile 117 Carmi Subdivision.
1944-12-14	Coquihalla Agreement cancelled.
1944-12-22	Railway Commission approved line between Haynes and Osoyoos for regular operation..
1944-12-28	Last spike on Osoyoos line driven in ceremony at Osoyoos. This was the last extension on the KVR.
1945-04-09	CPR announced it had purchased the GN line between Princeton and Brookmere for $1.5 million.

△ FIGURE 7-23 *The Copper Mountain mine reopened in June 1937 after a seven-year closure and soon became an important contributor to Canada's war production. In this picture 3506 pulls a train of ore cars through the dump to the concentrator mill at Allenby after the mine's reopening.* PHOTO BY BILL PRESLEY. COLLECTION OF BILL PRESLEY

▽ FIGURE 7-24 *The Second World War placed restrictions on materials and manpower, but the KVR was permitted to build a new station at its railway yard in Penticton to replace the original lakeshore station. By being able to eliminate the run down to the lakeshore station and back the KVR was able to shorten the running time of Trains 11 and 12 by half an hour in each direction. This picture shows the new station shortly after its opening on December 15, 1941. An addition was built to the east side after the Second World War.* PENTICTON MUSEUM — STOCKS FAMILY COLLECTION

he Second Mainline

The Kettle Valley Railway: 1946-1959

THE LARGE AMOUNT OF TRAFFIC HANDLED ON THE KVR DURING THE WAR CONVINCED THE CPR THAT ITS KETTLE Valley Division would remain one of its most important divisions after war ended in 1945. In January 1946, with wartime rationing and restrictions ended, the CPR announced that it would immediately undertake an ambitious program to make the KVR of a standard equivalent to that of the company's mainline. All wooden trestles on the line would be renewed or eliminated by fills or steel structures. All ties would be replaced. A major upgrading would be made on the line between Princeton and Brookmere, acquired from the GN only a few months earlier. The GN had been unwilling to improve this line under its ownership, but now the CPR was free to go ahead. As part of this work a new tunnel was constructed and the line relocated for a short section along the east bank of the Tulameen River five miles west of Princeton to eliminate the need to replace two of the five wooden Howe Truss bridges on the former GN line.

The CPR also continued its wartime policy of keeping the Coquihalla line open for as much of the year as possible. Bulldozers were introduced for snowfighting. The power and flexibility of these machines proved superior to the use of rotary and wing plows, and as a consequence the CPR decided to remove all but five of the original 15 snowsheds on the line. At Mile 28.2, where it was decided to retain a snowshed, a new shed was built of concrete. Major improvements were undertaken on other parts of the Coquihalla Subdivision as well.

The CPR's large capital investment in the KVR was supported by substantial freight traffic. The Trail smelter in particular continued to ship a large portion of its output over the KVR for export from Vancouver, or its affiliate Pacific Coast Terminals in New Westminster. Fruit traffic grew so much that on April 27, 1947 the CPR introduced a new daily train service between Penticton and Vancouver, Trains 45 and 46. Although the transport of fruit was the prime purpose for the new trains, a coach and sleeper were added to the end of each train to complement the service offered by Trains 11 and 12.

To handle both the new express service and the steady growth in other freight traffic, the CPR supplemented the P1 class 5100 series 2-8-2 steam locomotives with P2 class 5200 series locomotives of the same wheel arrangement. Early in 1949 oil

◁ FIGURE 8-1 *The 15-year period immediately following the Second World War produced significant change on the Kettle Valley Railway. Continued upgrading of the line, the introduction of diesel-electric locomotives and the heavy movement of through freight traffic earned the railway the title "The Second Mainline." Here a pair of newly introduced Canadian Locomotive Company diesels lift a heavy freight up the grade through the tunnel at Mile 23.5 (Coquihalla Subdivision) and across the frame trestle at Mile 23.3.* COURTESY CANADIAN PACIFIC CORPORATE ARCHIVES (M5987)

FIGURE 8-2

▷ FIGURE 8-2
Engine 5134
passes Hope station on
its way eastbound with a
freight in 1948. The tail
of the train is still on
the Fraser River bridge.
PHOTO BY NORM GIDNEY

tanks were erected at Penticton, Princeton, Midway and Brookmere to allow these and other Kettle Valley Division steam locomotives to burn oil fuel. But oil-fired steam locomotives would enjoy only brief service on the line. In September 1951 the CPR tested the first diesel-electric locomotive over the KVR. More tests followed that fall. Impressed with the results, the CPR announced in 1952 that it had committed a program to convert the Kootenay Division and Kettle Valley Division entirely to diesel power. In May 1953 the diesel units started to arrive in large numbers, and by the end of summer few steam locomotives were left on either division.

As well as introducing diesels, the CPR undertook a major passenger train schedule improvement in April 1952 in an effort to counter the severe loss of passenger patronage experienced following the November 1949 opening of the Hope-Princeton Highway. Unfortunately, the improvements were to no avail in stemming the public drift away from the railway. Fruit traffic between Penticton and the coast was also lost to truck competition over the new highway. As a consequence, in September 1954 the CPR discontinued Trains 45 and 46, the fruit express and passenger service introduced in 1947.

Patronage on remaining passenger Trains 11 and 12 dwindled. In October 1957 the CPR resurrected the numbers Train 45 and 46 for passenger train service on the KVR, but dropped the train names and downgraded the service to coach only. All express, sleeping car and dining car service was discontinued. Mixed train service on the Merritt branch was dropped at the same time. The CPR had planned to introduce Budd Cars for the service to allow an accelerated schedule, but the cars were delayed in delivery from the manufacturer and the revised service was commenced with a single diesel unit, baggage car and coach.

The promised Budd Cars were introduced to regular service in March 1958. However, a month earlier the CPR had cut passenger train service between Nelson and Penticton to only twice per week, and had revised schedules so that eastbound passengers had a night layover at both Penticton and Nelson. Westbound through passengers had a night layover at Nelson. The Board of Transport Commissioners conducted several public hearings into complaints about the cutbacks, but concluded that the patronage losses had preceded any cutbacks and had occurred despite numerous attempts by the company in the early 1950s to make the service attractive.

M841 Mon.	43 Daily	11 Daily	Miles	TABLE 151 —cont'd	Altitude	12 Daily	44 Daily	M842 Wed.
A.M.	P.M.	A.M.				P.M.	P.M.	P.M.
7.00	6.05	11..	0.0	Lv NELSON ‖155.158 PT Ar	1763	4.55	12.25	5.25
f7.12	f6.15	f11.59	4.7	..Taghum..	1756	f4.41	12.10	5.07
f7.19	6.20	12.05	7.1	..Beasley..	1759	f4.36	12.05	5.00
f7.30	f6.27	12.12	7.1	..Bonnington..	1686	f4.29	f11.57	4.50
7.35	6.31	12.17	11.9	..SOUTH SLOCAN 158..	1623	4.26	11.53	4.46
A.M.	f6.37	12.25	14.3	..Shoreacres..	526	f4.19	f11.46	P.M.
..	f6.40	12.28	15.6	..Glade..	528	f4.16	f11.43	
..	6.45	12.32	17.9	..Tarrys..	528	f4.11	f11.38	
..	6.49	12.36	19.9	..Thrums..	503	4.07	f11.34	
..	6.57	12.44	23.5	..Brilliant..	1446	4.00	f11.27	
..	7.05	12•49	25.7	..Castlegar ┼155..	1432	3.53	11.20	
..	P.M.	1.10	27.4	..Robson West..	1408	f3.40	A.M.	
..	1.19	32.4	..Labarthe..	1412	f3.30			
..	1.42	39.1	..Shields..	2041	3.13			
..	1.55	43.6	..Coykendahl..	2531	f3.02			
..	2.14	50.4	..Tunnel..	3221	f2.42			
..	2.30	55.1	..Porcupine..	3674	f2.30			
..	2.41	58.0	..Farron..	3976	2.22			
..	2.54	62.4	..Paulson..	3346	f2.02			
..	3.05	66.4	..Coryell..	3120	f1.50			
..	3.20	70.4	..Lafferty..	2656	f1.38			
..	3.39	76..	..Fife..	1974	1.15			
..	f3.52	81.8	..Cascade..	1577	12.56			
..	3.55	82.8	..Billings..	.642	f12.49			
..	f4.05	87.1	..Gilpin..	1669	f12.41			
..	4.21	94.7	..Grand Forks..	1733	12.25			
..	4.24	95.3	Ar..City Jct..Lv	1733	12.18			
..	4.33	1.6	Ar Grand Forks City Lv		12.08			
..	4.54	95.3	Lv..City Jct..Ar	1733	f11.58			
..	5.10	100.3	..Fisherman..	2229	f11.48			
..	5.37	108.1	..Eholt..	3087	f11.20			
..	6.03	117.3	..GREENWOOD..	2454	11.01			
..	6.12	121.0	..Boundary Falls..	2333	f10.48			
..	6.25	126.4	Lv..MIDWAY..Lv	1903	10.35			
..	6.40	126.6	Lv..MIDWAY..Ar	1903	10.35			
..	6.58	133.5	..Kettle Valley..	951	f10.05			
..	7.07	138.5	..Rock Creek..	1978	10.00			
..	7.22	145.6	..Zamora..	2047	f9.46			
..	7.37	151.4	..Westbridge..	2051	f9.43			
..	f7.52	158.0	..Rhone..	2139	f9.36			
..	f7.52	158.0	..Taurus..	2342	f9.24			
..	8.13	168.9	..Beaverdell..	2582	9.04			
..	8.30	173.2	..Carmi..	2778	8.54			
..	8.50	180.8	..Lois..	3134	f8.35			
..	9.08	187.6	..Lakevale..	3454	f8.22			
..	f9.33	196.9	..Cookson..	3885	f8.05			
..	9.50	203.2	..McCulloch..	4150	f7.53			
..	f10.05	210.6	..Myra..	4160	f7.37			
..	f10.25	217.8	..Ruth..	1978	f7.31			
..	f10.40	224.2	..Lorna..	4035	f7.02			
..	f10.50	233..	..Chute Lake..	3907	f6.45			
45 Daily	f11.15	239.8	..Adra..	3220	f6.22	46 Daily		
..	f11.31	245.6	..Glenfir..	2585	f6.03			
..	f11.55	252.3	..Arawana..	1856	f5.44			
P.M.	12.20	260.3	Ar PENTICTON 157┼Lv	1120	5.20	A.M.		
8.30	12.50	260.3	Lv PENTICTON 157┼Ar	1120	4.55	7.10		
f8.53	1.04	267.3	..Winslow..	1508	f4.33	6.50		
9.04	1.17	269.8	..West Summerland..	1715	4.20	6.40		
9.20	1.32	275.8	..Faulder..	2198	f4.07	6.28		
9.48	f2.12	286.0	..Kirton..	2985	f3.45	6.06		
f10.05	f2.30	292.7	..Thirsk..	3307	f3.19	5.40		
f10.17	f3.05	298.8	..Osprey Lake..	3592	f3.05	5.25		
f10.31	f3.05	306.0	..Jellicoe..	3338	f3.05	5.25		
f10.46	3.22	313.6	..Erris..	3217	f2.50	5.10		
f11.00	f3.36	320.4	..Jura..	3051	f2.37	4.57		
f11.12	f3.48	325.5	..Belfort..	2545	f2.20	4.40		
11.25	4.15	330.8	..Princeton..	2126	1.55	4.25		
f12.05	f4.35	342.4	..Coalmont..	2126	1.19	3.44		
12.25	4.46	346.4	..Tulameen..	2502	1.05	3.37	M808 Mon.	
M807 Sun.								
A.M.							A.M.	
9.00	12.50	5.00	353.2	..Manning..	2574	f12.50	3.15	10.40
..	1.15	5.20	363.2	..Thalia..	2840	f12.30	2.55	
..	1.25	5.25	365.2	..Spearing..	2950	12.26	2.51	
1.30	5.35	369.2	Ar..Brookmere 154..Lv	3157	f12.20	2.45		
1.45	5.50	368.9	Lv..Brookmere 154..Ar	3157	12.05	2.30		
..	5.58	372.9	..Brodie..	3028	f11.57			
2.09	6.10	378.7	..Juliet..	3298	f11.44	2.09		
7.32	6.35	386.9	..Coquihalla..	3658	f11.26	1.48		
2.50	6.53	393.0	..Romeo..	3033	f11.00	1.25		
3.07	7.10	398.5	..Iago..	2423	f10.34	12.50		
3.22	7.26	403.3	..Portia..	1917	f10.15	12.40		
3.40	7.40	408.7	..Jessica..	1307	f9.58	12.23		
3.52	7.53	414.1	..Lear..	780	f9.39	12.04		
4.05	8.08	417.8	..Othello..	578	f9.30	f11.55		
4.05	8.20	423.2	..Hope..	110	9.15	f11.45		
2.05	4.25	8.35	425.5	Ar..Odlum 7..Lv	182	9.00	11.35	5.40
2.15	f4.31	8.42	428.5	..Katz 7..	110	9.00	11.35	5.15
..	7.15	11.45	512.8	Ar VANCOUVER ‖┼7..Lv	14	5.50	8.45	
P.M.	A.M.			PT		A.M.		

EXPLANATION OF SIGNS THIS PAGE

• Daily.
† Daily ex. Sun.
‖ Meal Station.
△ Breakfast stop.
★ Regularly assigned cars AIR-CONDITIONED.
┼ C.P. Air Lines Service to and from Calgary, Cranbrook, Castlegar, Penticton and Vancouver.
● Connects with Bus to and from Trail.
d Stops to detrain from west of Castlegar.
g Stops on signal.
g Stops on signal from west of Midway.
k Stops on signal Sat. only.
M Mixed Train.
w Stops to detrain from Swift Current and east, also entrain for west of Lethbridge.
E.T. Eastern Time.
C.T. Central Time.
M.T. Mountain Time.
P.T. Pacific Time.

EQUIPMENT
S.I. 1
Yahk-Spokane
Coaches
Yahk-Spokane
S.I. 2
Spokane-Yahk
Coaches
Spokane-Yahk.
Nos. 511-512
Medicine Hat-Lethbridge
Coaches
Sleeper
12-1 (ex. Sat.)
Regina to Lethbridge.
(Handled in train 7 Regina to Medicine Hat)
12-1 (Ex. Sun.)
Lethbridge to Regina.
(Handled in train 8 Medicine Hat to Regina.)
Nos. 681-682
Lethbridge-Yahk
Coaches

EQUIPMENT—No. 11—KOOTENAY EXPRESS—Medicine Hat to Vancouver.
★Coach..........Medicine Hat to Vancouver.
★Sleeper, 12-1...Calgary to Vancouver (*In train 542 Calgary to MacLeod*).
★Sleeper, 12-1...Lethbridge to Nelson (Dec. 4 to Jan. 15) (Open 9.45 p.m.).
★Cafe Parlor.....Calgary to Penticton. (*In train 542 Calgary to MacLeod*).
★Diner..........Hope to Vancouver.
No. 12—KETTLE VALLEY EXPRESS—Vancouver to Medicine Hat.
★Coach..........Vancouver to Medicine Hat.
★Sleeper, 12-1...Vancouver to Calgary (*In train 541 MacLeod to Calgary*).
★Sleeper, 12-1...Nelson to Lethbridge (Dec. 5 to Jan. 16).
★Cafe Parlor.....Penticton to Calgary. (*In train 541 MacLeod to Calgary*).
★Diner..........Vancouver to Hope.
Nos. 45-46—Between Vancouver and Penticton.
Sleeper, (12 Sec., D.R.) (*Occupancy until 8.00 a.m.*)
Sleeper, (1 D.R., 4 Cpts.) (*Occupancy until 8.00 a.m.*)

FIGURE 8-3 COLLECTION OF BARRIE SANFORD

☐ FIGURES 8-3 & 8-4 *In the early postwar period Canadian Pacific undertook many improvements to its Kettle Valley Division. FIGURE 8-3 from a 1948 CPR public timetable shows through passenger Trains 11 and 12, and newly introduced Trains 45 and 46 between Vancouver and Penticton. The twice weekly service between Brookmere and Spences Bridge shown in FIGURE 8-4 would be improved to three times per week in September 1949.*

BROOKMERE — SPENCE'S BRIDGE

M805 Tue. & Fri.	Miles	TABLE 154	M806 Wed. & Sat.
A.M.		Pacific Time	P.M.
6.00	0.0	Lv..Brookmere 151..Lv	1.35
6.13	4.0	....Brodie....	1.20
6.40	11.6	...Kingsvale...	12.40
f 7.05	20.0	..Glen Walker..	12.00
8.50	29.4	Ar...Merritt...Lv	11.15
8.55		Ar...Nicola...Lv	11.00
		Lv...Nicola...Ar	10.30
	29.4	Lv...Merritt...Ar	10.05
f 9.15	31.5	....Coutlee....	f 9.55
f 9.37	34.2	....Coyle....	f 9.42
f10.01	39.9	...Canford...	f 9.23
f10.40	48.9	....Dot....	f 8.53
f10.52	51.9	....Agate....	f 8.38
f11.20	59.1	..Clapperton..	f 8.20
12.00	69.2	Ar..SPENCE'S BRIDGE 7..Lv	7.45
NOON			A.M.

FIGURE 8-4
COLLECTION OF BARRIE SANFORD

FIGURE 8-5

▷ FIGURE 8-5 *Another major improvement undertaken to the Kettle Valley Railway in the postwar decade was the introduction of diesel-electric locomotives. On September 2, 1951 the Canadian Locomotive Company two-unit diesel "City of Kingston" made the first run of a diesel locomotive on the KVR, running from Midway to Penticton with a regular freight train. The following day it ran through to Vancouver. Here fireman Dawson Raincock stands in front of the lead locomotive at Brookmere after bringing the engine from Penticton. He is smiling in this pose, perhaps little realizing that within two years steam locomotives would be virtually gone from the Kettle Valley Railway and the role of fireman rendered obsolete.* COLLECTION OF JOE SMUIN

▷ FIGURES 8-6 & 8-7
In April 1952 the CPR undertook a bold rescheduling of passenger train service on the KVR in an effort to regain the substantial loss of ridership following the opening of the Hope-Princeton Highway in Novermber 1949. Trains 11 and 12 were rescheduled to operate between Vancouver and Penticton during daylight hours. The schedule change opened spectacular Coquihalla Pass to daytime viewing, and offered both daytime and overnight service between Vancouver and Penticton with complementing night Trains 45 and 46. Unfortunately, the improved service failed to stem the general drift of passengers to road and airline competition. FIGURE 8-6 shows engine 5258 piloting Train 12 around the curve on the upper Jura loop at Mile 62.5 (Princeton Subdivision). The short train confirms the diminished passenger ridership.

FIGURE 8-7 shows sister Train 11, with a 5200 series "Mikado" for motive power, crossing Ladner Creek bridge at Mile 36.8 (Coquihalla Subdivision) on the new daylight schedule.

The Board concluded the railway's actions were justified. Daily service remained in place between Vancouver and Penticton, twice per week east of the latter point.

The decline in Kettle Valley Railway passenger traffic during the late 1950s did not provide an accurate measure of the railway's general status at the time. Passenger travel by rail was on the wane all over North America throughout the decade, and even with this loss the KVR remained a busy railway. Freight trains leaving Penticton for the coast with four headend diesels and a sling of "pushers" were a common sight in the late 1950s, as the output of the Kootenay mines rolled westward in increasing tonnages.

The heavy through traffic finally confirmed the original purpose of the line's construction: the Coast-to-Kootenay railway. By 1959 the Kettle Valley Railway was no longer merely a branch line feeding traffic to the Canadian Pacific mainline. With the improvements undertaken in the late 1940s and 1950s the KVR had become equal in physical standard to any of the single track portions of the CPR mainline in the province, and second only to the mainline in traffic volume. Indeed, the Kettle Valley Railway had become "The Second Mainline."

FIGURES 8-8, 8-9, 8-10 *Nicholas Morant, widely recognized as the premier corporate photographer of the CPR, took these three fine pictures as part of a series of publicity pictures marking the introduction of diesel locomotives to KVR passenger train service in May 1953. FIGURE 8-8 shows Train 12 along the shore of Otter Lake west of Tulameen. FIGURES 8-9 and 8-10 show passenger trains on the 560-foot-long steel bridge over Ladner Creek at Mile 36.8 (Coquihalla Subdivision). The 12° 36' curve of the bridge is more evident in these two pictures than in FIGURE 8-7 taken a year earlier.*

FIGURE 8-11

△ FIGURE 8-11 *Three CLC built diesels pull a heavy eastbound freight up the grade from Penticton towards Arawana in September 1954. The locomotives are obviously working hard, but the train they are pulling is more than double the length which would have been handled with steam locomotives, even using several "pushers."* PHOTO BY ANDRE MORIN

▷ FIGURE 8-12 *New and old: Less than six months after leaving the Canadian Locomotive Company shops in April 1954 diesel engine 4104 stands nose to nose with steam locomotive 5212 in Penticton yard on September 26, 1954 as 5212 prepares to leave Penticton for the final time.* PENTICTON MUSEUM — STOCKS FAMILY COLLECTION

FIGURE 8-12

▷ FIGURE 8-13 *Engine 5212's dramatic display of steam and smoke as it leaves Penticton on the morning of September 26, 1954 is perhaps symbolic. The engine is leaving for Vancouver with the last steam-powered train to operate on the Kettle Valley Railway, discounting a few work trains on the Coquihalla line and the Provincial Museum train in 1977. The Kettle Valley Division had been fully dieselized for approximately a year at this time. Steam operation on the KVR was limited to overnight Trains 45 and 46 operating between Vancouver and Penticton with steam locomotives from Port Coquitlam. With the timetable taking effect earlier that morning these two trains were discontinued. Thus engine 5212 was returning to Port Coquitlam for the final time.* PENTICTON MUSEUM — STOCKS FAMILY COLLECTION

FIGURE 8-14

FIGURE 8-15

△ FIGURE 8-14
When this fine picture of Train 12 crossing Trout Creek bridge west of Penticton was taken in September 1954, the train had already assumed much of the express function of complementing Trains 45 and 46, as evidenced by the numerous fruit express cars on the train. Trains 45 and 46 were by this time operating only Monday to Friday and would be discontinued before the end of that same month.
PHOTO BY ANDRE MORIN

◁ FIGURE 8-15 *In this interesting photo taken on the Coquihalla line just east of Romeo, an eastbound freight train is passing through 220-foot-long Tunnel 6 at Mile 23.5 and is starting over the trestle being filled between there and Tunnel 5 at Mile 23.1. At the west portal of Tunnel 6 is an emergency water supply flume originally intended for steam locomotives, but left in place for diesels overtaxed by the 2.2% grade leading up to Coquihalla.*
COURTESY CANADIAN PACIFIC CORPORATE ARCHIVES (M5985)

FIGURE 8-16

◁ FIGURE 8-16 *The permanent closure of the Granby mine at Copper Mountain in April 1957 spelled the end for the Copper Mountain Subdivision. By July of that year salvaging of mine equipment had been completed and shortly afterwards dismantling of the line began. In this picture a work train salvages steel and timber from the 765-foot-long trestle across Smelter Flat at Mile 10.0.*
COLLECTION OF BARRIE SANFORD

FIGURE 8-17 COLLECTION OF BARRIE SANFORD

FIGURE 8-18 COLLECTION OF BILL PRESLEY

☐ FIGURES 8-17, 8-18, 8-19 *Through the postwar period continued improvements were made on the Coquihalla line. FIGURE 8-17 shows steel girders being positioned to replace the 315-foot-long wooden trestle over Tack Creek at Mile 21.7 (Coquihalla Subdivision) in July 1954.*

FIGURE 8-18 shows a diversion built around Tunnel 4 at Mile 22.5 (Coquihalla Subdivision) after the west portal was plugged by a major rockslide in May 1959. In reality the diversion's life was brief, as within six months the last train ran over the Coquihalla line. This view of the plugged tunnel and new line was taken from a westbound train.

FIGURE 8-19 is looking eastward from inside Tunnel 7 at Mile 27.6 (Coquihalla Subdivision).

FIGURE 8-19 COLLECTION OF BARRIE SANFORD

Kettle Valley Railway Dateline

1946 - 1959

1947-01-09 Tender of Engine 5172 fell into turntable pit at Penticton.

1947-04-27 Trains 45 and 46 between Vancouver and Penticton introduced.

1948-03-29 Engine 5213 and several cars of westbound freight derailed by rockslide along shore of Otter Lake.

1948-05-03 Railway Commission approved CPR plan for construction of a new line along the east bank of the Tulameen River between Mile 75.2 and 76.0 (Princeton Subdivision), eliminating bridges at Mile 75.2 and Mile 75.5, and involving the construction of a 484-foot-long tunnel at Mile 75.8.

1949-03-21 Engine 907 blew boiler inside roundhouse at Brookmere. One killed.

1949-09-25 Passenger service on Merritt Subdivision increased from twice per week to three times per week.

1949-11-26 Foundation of bridge at Mile 28.4 (Merritt Subdivision) undermined by high water. Passengers transferred across bridge on foot for three weeks.

1949-11-29 Engine 5261 of Train 12 derailed by washout just east of Penticton.

1949-12-21 Eight cars of cattle broke loose from Merritt yard and ran downgrade into an eastbound freight at Coyle. Yard engine giving chase to cars smashed into wreckage. One killed.

1950-04-30 Sunday service on Trains 45 and 46 discontinued.

1950-10-14 Trains 11 and 12 collided at Jellicoe. Engine 5221 on Train 11 and 5121 on Train 12 derailed.

1951-01-25 Snowslide smashed out snowshed at Mile 28.2 (Coquihalla Subdivision). Snowshed was rebuilt of concrete.

1951-09-02 Canadian Locomotive Company two-unit diesel "City of Kingston" made test run from Midway to Penticton and the following day ran from Penticton to Vancouver. First diesel locomotive operated over the KVR.

1952-01-09 Train 11 arrived in Vancouver with first diesel-powered passenger train operated over KVR.

1952-04-27 Major passenger train schedule change. Trains 11 and 12 became day trains west of Penticton, complementing overnight Trains 45 and 46.

1952-10-18 CPR announced it had ordered 73 diesel locomotives to replace steam locomotives on the Kootenay and Kettle Valley Divisions.

1953-07-06 First diesel locomotive operated over the Copper Mountain Subdivision.

1953-08-18 First diesel locomotive operated over the Merritt Subdivision.

1954-01-28 Train 12 ran into snowslide near Iago. Engine 4083 derailed and slid 150 feet down into canyon. Three injured.

1954-04-25 Saturday service on Trains 45 and 46 discontinued.

1954-09-26 Trains 45 and 46 discontinued. Engine 5212 ran from Penticton to Vancouver with the last official run of a steam locomotive on the KVR.

1955-04-24 KVR passenger trains renumbered Trains 67 and 68.

1955-10-08 Westbound freight ran into rear of passenger Train 67 stopped at Osprey Lake. Two killed. Engine 4077 leading freight scrapped after incident.

1956-10-14 Engine 8903 and several cars of passenger Train 67 derailed at Mile 82.8 (Carmi Subdivision).

1957-04-30 Copper Mountain mine permanently closed.

1957-05-13 Coalmont station destroyed by fire.

1957-07-19 Last train operated from Copper Mountain.

1957-07-26 Canadian Transport Commission approved abandonment of Copper Mountain Subdivision.

1957-10-27 KVR passenger trains renumbered 45 and 46 and downgraded to coach only. Mixed train service between Spences Bridge and Brookmere discontinued.

1958-02-03 Last day of daily passenger train service between Penticton and Nelson. Service reduced to twice per week each way after this date.

Dateline cont'd.

1958-02-07	Budd Car 9022 made test run from Nelson to Vancouver.
1958-03-03	Budd Car 9197 operated Vancouver to Nelson with first Budd Car run carrying passengers. Thereafter only Budd Cars were used in passenger service except during emergency conditions.
1959-04-18	Engines 8715, 8548, 4454 and 4064 of freight train derailed at Mile 37.5 (Princeton Subdivision).
1959-05-11	Tunnel 4 Mile 22.5 (Coquihalla Subdivision) collapsed. Diversion subsequently built.
1959-06-17	Andrew McCulloch Memorial in Gyro Park at Penticton unveiled.
1959-10-28	Eleven freight cars derailed at Osprey Lake.
1959-11-23	Coquihalla Subdivision badly damaged by slides and washouts. Line never reopened. The last train over the entire line was eastbound freight the evening before, engines 4079, 8725, 8714 and 4064. The last passenger train was Train 45, Budd Car 9197, the day previous.

FIGURE 8-20

◁ FIGURE 8-20 *Rail Diesel Cars — commonly called Budd Cars — took over passenger service on the KVR starting in March 1958. The white lights and flags on this Budd Car exiting from the eastern Quintette Tunnel at Othello indicate that the train is a Passenger Extra. The date is September 19, 1959 and the train is running behind regular Train 46 carrying members of the Rail Travel League on a day outing from Vancouver to Coquihalla and return. Little did the passengers realize they were among the last to make the journey; two months later a train ride through Coquihalla Pass would no longer be possible.* PHOTO BY ANDRE MORIN

▷ FIGURE 8-21 *Tracks lie suspended in midair across a washout at Mile 38.3 (Coquihalla Subdivision) in November 1959. This was one of several severe disruptions which prompted the Canadian Pacific Railway to abandon "The Second Mainline."* COLLECTION OF BILL PRESLEY

FIGURE 8-21

CHAPTER 9

And Gone So Soon

The Kettle Valley Railway: 1960-1964

ONE DAY — NOVEMBER 23, 1959 — CHANGED THE DESTINY OF RAILROADING IN SOUTHERN BRITISH COLUMBIA. Early that morning the CPR dispatcher in Penticton received a telephone call that a washout had occurred at Mile 43 of the Coquihalla Subdivision. By daybreak it had been discovered that there were three additional washouts on the line, all of them severe. The following day an even larger washout occurred at Mile 38.3. On November 28 the CPR announced that the line would be closed temporarily until the unseasonably wet weather had abated and the damage could be repaired. In the meantime passenger Trains 45 and 46 would be diverted to a connection with mainline passenger trains at Spences Bridge. Freight trains would likewise divert over the Merritt line.

The following spring the rail line through Coquihalla Pass still had not been reopened. In fact, throughout all of 1960 Coquihalla Pass was devoid of the customary sounds of railroading. On January 9, 1961 the CPR issued a brief and stoic press announcement officially stating what many people had already come to suspect: the CPR did not intend to reopen the Coquihalla line. The press release stated that because of the cost of repairing the damage — estimated at $251,000 — the CPR had decided to abandon the line. It was curtain call for the Coquihalla.

Although the CPR announcement was not a surprise when it was made, it seemed inexplicably peculiar. An outlay of $251,000 was hardly a large expenditure. Indeed, considering the heavy investment which the company had made in improving the Coquihalla line during the 1940s and 1950s — including the expenditure of more than half a million dollars in 1959 — the refusal to allocate $251,000 for repairs was contradictory to the long term program established by the CPR in the early postwar years.

But the damage of November 1959 was the catalyst which sparked a fundamental change in Canadian Pacific management philosophy concerning its rail network in southern British Columbia. The enormous expenditures on improvements to the Coquihalla line had not exempted the line from disruption. Further expenditures offered no assurance of improvement. Perhaps the Montreal managers of Canadian Pacific had finally come to concur with Alexander Mackenzie's assessment of the mountains of British Columbia as "a land of superlative difficulties." In any case, they decided that coastbound Kootenay freight would no longer be carried over the Kettle Valley

◁ FIGURE 9-1
Railroading in southern British Columbia changed dramatically when the rail line through Coquihalla Pass was abandoned and rail traffic patterns in the province significantly reoriented after the line was damaged by slides and washouts in November 1959. This picture looks eastward towards Hope station and Coquihalla Pass shortly after the trains had stopped running.
PHOTO BY BARRIE SANFORD

Railway. Instead, this traffic would be sent from the Kootenays north over the Lake Windermere Subdivision to Golden, then west over the CPR mainline, even though for much of this traffic the diversion added more than 330 miles to its journey. The limited amount of local traffic generated by the Boundary District and Okanagan could easily be sent to the coast via the Merritt line. Under this plan the Coquihalla line was redundant. It was no longer an integral link in the rail system of southern British Columbia.

In July 1961 the Board of Transport Commissioners granted the CPR approval to abandon the Coquihalla line. Work on salvaging rails and other material began within a few weeks, and was completed the following year. In itself the abandonment of the Coquihalla rail line would not have radically changed the character of the Kettle Valley Railway. After all, the KVR had often operated without the use of the line. However, the CPR decision to divert Kootenay freight traffic via the mainline had a devastating effect on the KVR. When the changeover took effect in September 1961 more than 80% of the KVR's freight traffic vanished in a single day. The 22 train crews based at Penticton were suddenly reduced to five. So little traffic was left that the following year the CPR formally abolished the Kettle Valley Division and assigned segments of the line to other divisions. In less than three years the Kettle Valley Railway had been transformed from its status as "The Second Mainline" to little more than a minor branch line.

The closure of the Coquihalla line devasted passenger traffic. The longer routing via Spences Bridge, with a forced change of trains in the middle of the night, resulted in the disappearance of the last vestiges of passenger trade. Permission to drop the service was granted, and on January 17, 1964 — one year short of half a century of passenger operation — the last passenger train journeyed over the Kettle Valley Railway.

▷ FIGURE 9-4 *The abandonment of the Coquihalla line ended travel on one of the world's most fascinating rail lines. No longer would rail travelers enjoy such magnificent vistas as this one of the Coquihalla River and Mount Hope looking westward at Othello. Gone too were the Shakespearian station names given the Coquihalla Pass railway by Andrew McCulloch.*
CANADIAN PACIFIC
CORPORATE ARCHIVES (M5695)

 FIGURES 9-2 & 9-3 *During 1961 CPR crews salvaged rails and other materials on the Coquihalla line from Boston Bar Creek westward to Hope. In 1962 crews worked eastward from Boston Bar Creek to Brodie. Here crews lift rails from the passing track at Iago during the summer of 1962. The water tank lies pushed over alongside the work train.*

FIGURE 9-4

▽ FIGURE 9-5 *This editorial appeared in the Vancouver Sun, April 6, 1961.*

And Gone So Soon

Forty-six years has been the life of the world's most expensive railroad.

They'll soon be tearing-up the tracks on the Kettle Valley line through Coquihalla Pass. Mile for mile, says the CPR, it was the most expensive ever built.

Perhaps it has never paid off for the railway company. But it has paid British Columbia well.

First planned in the early 1890's, it was not finished until 1915. In the meantime, the commercial empire of the Kootenay mines slipped away from Vancouver into the hands of Spokane, whose merchants and capitalists profited well by it.

Once the road was opened, It changed the Ellis cattle kingdom into the rich fruitlands of the present southern Okanagan. Bit by bit, Trail and the rich mines of southeastern B.C. were won back into the orbit of Canadian trade.

It was a costly line to maintain in money and in lives. "They rode her down standing up," is the epitaph of more than one KVR train crew that never arrived at the other end of the canyon.

Good roads and fast trucks spelled the end of the canyon line. But they haven't wiped out the debt B.C. owes the men who built the world's most expensive railroad.

FIGURE 9-5

▷ FIGURE 9-6
Coquihalla salvage crews left any structures not economic to remove. This included the major steel bridge at Ladner Creek. The bridge still stands, and with careful inspection can be seen through the trees upstream of the Ladner Creek crossing on the Coquihalla Highway. PHOTO BY BARRIE SANFORD

▽ FIGURES 9-7 & 9-8
These two pictures show two of the snowsheds on the Coquihalla line following abandonment. The wooden snowshed shown in FIGURE 9-7 is the 290-foot-long snowshed at Mile 26.9 (originally designated Shed 14), one of only five snowsheds retained following the introduction of bulldozers for snowfighting in the late 1940s. The concrete snowshed in FIGURE 9-8 is at Mile 28.3 and was the only concrete snowshed on the KVR.

FIGURE 9-6

FIGURE 9-7 PHOTO BY BARRIE SANFORD

FIGURE 9-8 PHOTO BY BARRIE SANFORD

FIGURES 9-9 & 9-11 *Budd Cars continued to provide passenger train service on the Kettle Valley Railway following closure of the Coquihalla line. In FIGURE 9-9 Budd Cars 9022 and 9196 sit next to diesel engine 4065 in Penticton yard. In FIGURE 9-11 Budd Car 9022 appears almost diminutive as it crosses Trout Creek bridge with Train 46 for Penticton. The longer routing and the forced transfer between trains at Spences Bridge in the middle of the night virtually destroyed all passenger patronage.*

FIGURE 9-10 *This view is looking north along the Coquihalla line towards the level crossing with the Canadian National mainline at Hope in 1962. Out of the picture to the left is the interchange track used to allow CPR or CNR mainline passenger trains to cross to the opposite mainline when disruptions closed either line through the Fraser Canyon. This track was left in place at the time of the Coquihalla abandonment into Hope in 1961, but was removed in 1963. The remainder of KVR track was removed in 1970.* PHOTO BY BARRIE SANFORD

FIGURE 9-12

NELSON—PENTICTON—VANCOUVER

♥45 Dayliner Mon., Thu.	Miles	TABLE 40	Altitude	♥46 ♦ Dayliner Tue., Fri.
READ DOWN				READ UP
A.M.				P.M.
9.00	0.0	Lv....NELSON PT......Ar	1763	5.05
....	4.7	........Taghum........	1756	....
....	7.1	........Beasley........	1759	....
....	10.4	.......Bonnington.......	1686	....
ƒ 9.24	11.9	.....SOUTH SLOCAN.....	1623	ƒ 4.41
ƒ 9.29	14.3	......Shoreacres......	1526	ƒ 4.36
ƒ 9.32	15.6	.........Glade.........	1528	ƒ 4.33
ƒ 9.38	19.9	........Thrums........	1503	ƒ 4.27
ƒ 9.44	23.5	.......Brilliant.......	1446	ƒ 4.21
9.50	25.7	Ar....Castlegar ✛....Lv	1432	4.17
		(See Table 34)		
⊙	..	Lv...Castlegar....Ar	..	⊙
⊙	..	Ar...Trail....Lv	..	⊙
9.50	25.7	Lv...Castlegar ✛....Ar	1432	4.17
		(See Table 34)		
..	27.4	.......Robson West.......	1408	..
ƒ10.16	32.4	.......Labarthe.......	1412	ƒ 3.49
ƒ10.27	39.1	.........Shields.........	2041	ƒ 3.38
ƒ10.42	43.5	......Coykendahl......	2531	ƒ 3.23
..	50.4	.........Tunnel.........	3221	..
..	55.1	.......Porcupine.......	3674	..
ƒ11.00	58.0	.........Farron.........	3976	ƒ 3.05
ƒ11.09	62.5	.........Paulson.........	3346	ƒ 2.56
ƒ11.16	66.4	.........Coryell.........	3120	ƒ 2.49
..	70.5	.......Lafferty.......	2656	..
ƒ11.38	76.9	..........Fife..........	1974	ƒ 2.27
ƒ11.49	81.8	.........Cascade.........	1577	ƒ 2.16
ƒ11.56	86.9	.........Gilpin.........	1669	ƒ 2.09
12.09	94.8	......Grand Forks......	1733	1.56
..	100.3	.......Fisherman.......	2229	..
ƒ12.39	108.7	..........Eholt..........	3087	ƒ 1.26
12.55	117.3	.......Greenwood.......	2454	1.10
..	121.0	......Boundary Falls......	2333	..
1.15	126.6	Ar.....MIDWAY.....Lv	1903	12.50
1.30	126.6	Lv.....MIDWAY.....Ar	1903	12.40
ƒ 1.43	135.5	......Kettle Valley......	1951	ƒ12.26
ƒ 1.47	138.3	.......Rock Creek.......	1978	ƒ12.22
ƒ 1.59	145.6	.........Zamora.........	2047	ƒ12.10
2.02	147.1	.......Westbridge.......	2051	12.07
ƒ 2.08	151.4	..........Rhone..........	2139	ƒ12.01
ƒ 2.19	158.0	.........Taurus.........	2342	ƒ11.51
ƒ 2.34	168.9	.......Beaverdell.......	2582	ƒ11.36
ƒ 2.41	173.2	..........Carmi..........	2778	ƒ11.28
ƒ 2.53	180.8	..........Lois..........	3134	ƒ11.17
ƒ 3.05	187.6	........Lakevale........	3454	ƒ11.04
ƒ 3.21	196.9	.........Cookson.........	3885	ƒ10.48
ƒ 3.31	203.2	.......McCulloch.......	4150	ƒ10.38
ƒ 3.45	210.6	..........Myra..........	4160	ƒ10.24
ƒ 4.02	217.8	..........Ruth..........	4090	ƒ10.09
ƒ 4.13	224.2	..........Lorna..........	4035	ƒ 9.58
ƒ 4.30	233.1	.......Chute Lake.......	3907	ƒ 9.42
ƒ 4.41	239.8	..........Adra..........	3220	ƒ 9.30
ƒ 4.53	245.5	.........Glenfir.........	2585	ƒ 9.19
ƒ 5.07	252.3	.........Arawana.........	1856	ƒ 9.07
c 5.25	260.3	Ar....PENTICTON 44 ✛....Lv	1120	e 8.50
P.M.				A.M.
Daily				Daily
P.M.				A.M.
6.45	260.3	Lv....PENTICTON 44 ✛......Ar	1120	8.00
ƒ 6.57	267.3	..........Winslow..........	1508	ƒ 7.47
7.03	269.8	.....West Summerland.....	1715	7.42
ƒ 7.13	275.8	..........Faulder..........	2198	ƒ 7.31
ƒ 7.29	286.0	..........Kirton..........	2985	ƒ 7.13
ƒ 7.40	292.7	..........Thirsk..........	3307	ƒ 7.03
ƒ 7.50	298.8	.......Osprey Lake.......	3592	ƒ 6.53
ƒ 8.01	306.0	..........Jellicoe..........	3338	ƒ 6.42
ƒ 8.12	313.6	...........Erris...........	3217	ƒ 6.31
ƒ 8.23	320.4	...........Jura...........	3051	ƒ 6.20
ƒ 8.32	325.5	..........Belfort..........	2545	ƒ 6.11
8.45	330.8	.........Princeton.........	2126	6.00
ƒ 9.06	342.5	.........Coalmont.........	2385	ƒ 5.38
ƒ 9.12	346.5	.........Tulameen.........	2502	ƒ 5.32
ƒ 9.21	353.3	..........Manning..........	2574	ƒ 5.22
ƒ 9.35	363.3	..........Thalia..........	2840	ƒ 5.08
ƒ 9.38	365.2	..........Spearing..........	2950	ƒ 5.05
9.45	368.9	Ar....Brookmere....Lv	3157	5.00
9.55	368.9	Lv....Brookmere....Ar	3157	4.55
..	372.9	..........Brodie..........	3028	..
..	398.3	..........Merritt..........	1960	..
11.59	438.1	Ar...SPENCE'S BRIDGE 7...Lv	774	2.50
P.M.				A.M.
7				8
A.M.				A.M.
12.30	438.1	Lv...SPENCE'S BRIDGE 7...Ar	774	2.35
7.15	615.8	Ar..VANCOUVER ✛ 7 ⊗ PT..Lv	14	8.10
A.M.				P.M.

EXPLANATION OF SIGNS—THIS PAGE

⊗ Meal Station where food and news supplies can be obtained at city prices.
♦ "The Canadian". All space reserved. No extra fare. ♥ Air-conditioned, R.D.C. (Rail Diesel Car). ✛ C.P. Air Lines Service to and from Calgary, Cranbrook, Castlegar, Penticton and Vancouver. ⊙ Taxi Service Available.
c Mon. and Thu. e Tue and Fri. ƒ Stops on signal.
E.T. Eastern Time. C.T. Central Time. M.T. Mountain Time. P.T. Pacific Time.

FIGURE 9-13

△ FIGURE 9-13 *Train order for the final run of Train 46 eastward from Spences Bridge on January 17, 1964.* COLLECTION OF BARRIE SANFORD

◁ FIGURE 9-12 *This schedule is from the CPR public timetable of October 27, 1963, the last timetable in which KVR passenger train service appeared prior to its discontinuation in January 1964. Note that the timetable does not show any train times at Merritt, nor any other stops on the line between Brodie and Spences Bridge. This absence was not an oversight. The CPR had cancelled its passenger tariff on the Merritt Subdivision when mixed train service was discontinued in 1957. Anticipating ultimate discontinuation of KVR passenger train service, the CPR did not seek Transport Commission approval for a new passenger tariff. Hence service could not be officially offered nor fares collected for travel on this section.* COLLECTION OF BARRIE SANFORD

FIGURE 9-14

▷ FIGURE 9-14 *Receipt for 40 cents received for a ticket on the last day of passenger train operation.* COLLECTION OF BARRIE SANFORD

Kettle Valley Railway Dateline

1960 - 1964

1961-02-25 Five cars of westbound freight derailed at Merritt. This was the last significant mishap on the KVR.

1961-07-18 Board of Transport Commissioners approved abandonment of Coquihalla Subdivision.

1961-09-01 Through freight traffic between coast and Kootenay points routed via Windermere Subdivision rather than KVR effective this date.

1961-10-29 All trackage between Penticton and Spences Bridge combined into the Princeton Subdivision.

1962-07-01 Kettle Valley Division abolished.

1962-10-24 Last spike removed from Coquihalla line.

1963-08-23 Board of Transport Commissioners authorized CPR to remove interchange with CN at Hope.

1963-10-23 Board of Transport Commissioners authorized CPR to discontinue passenger Trains 45 and 46 effective 1964-01-16.

1964-01-16 Budd Car left Spences Bridge with last official run of Train 46. Plow train ran ahead from Merritt, but passenger train arrived at Penticton 6 hours 10 minutes late. Train carried large group from West Summerland to Penticton who wanted to be on board "The Last Train." Budd Car returned to Spences Bridge that evening as Train 45.

1964-01-17 Train 46, Budd Car 9100, made last passenger train run from Spences Bridge to Penticton. At Penticton Budd Car 9100 was joined by 9022 and the two cars ran through to Midway and Nelson. This was the last passenger train to operate on the KVR, excepting excursion trains in 1983 and 1984.

FIGURE 9-15

FIGURE 9-15 *Budd Cars 9100 and 9022 wait at Penticton station ready to leave for Midway with the final run of Train 46. With the exception of passenger excursion trains operated to Penticton on the Victoria Day weekend in 1983 and 1984 this was the last passenger train to run over the tracks of the former Kettle Valley Railway.* COURTESY OF PENTICTON HERALD

emnant Railroad

The Kettle Valley Railway: 1965-1988

THE DISCONTINUATION OF THROUGH FREIGHT AND PAS-
SENGER SERVICE ON THE KVR LEFT ONLY WAY-FREIGHTS
and the occasional work train or special movement to traverse the
tracks of what only a few years earlier had been "The Second
Mainline." As of early 1964 way-freights ran three times per week each way between
Midway and Penticton, between Penticton and Brookmere, and between Brookmere
and Merritt. In August 1966 Brookmere was closed as a terminal point, after which
the tri-weekly way-freight west of Penticton ran through to Merritt. Service between
Merritt and Spences Bridge was daily except Saturday and Sunday, with the train handling local traffic from the sawmills of Merritt on those days when there was no traffic
to or from Penticton.

In April of 1966 a number of trains were diverted over the KVR as a result of
a closure of the CPR mainline near Revelstoke. The introduction of heavier "second
generation" diesels into mainline service later that year dictated that trackage on the
KVR would have to be maintained to a high standard if future diversions were to be
accommodated. The CPR considered the matter, and also studied the KVR in its plans
for handling the large volumes of Crowsnest coal which it had contracted to carry
to the coast starting in 1970. But the KVR had been built with the objective of carrying Boundary and West Kootenay traffic to the coast. For traffic from the Crowsnest
the distance and grade factors simply ruled out use of "The KV." As a consequence
Crowsnest coal was routed to the coast via the Windermere Valley line and the CPR
mainline. Track maintenance on the KVR was set in reflection of branchline status.
Within a few years mainline trains were no longer diverted over the KVR.

In the early 1970s the line enjoyed a surge in originating traffic resulting from
the opening of large and modern sawmills at both Princeton and Okanagan Falls. Some
traffic also came to the KVR — sadly perhaps — as a result of the discontinuation of
CPR barge service on Okanagan Lake at the end of May 1972. To handle this traffic
Canadian Pacific — now using the corporate name CP Rail — commenced operating
freight trains straight through between Penticton and Spences Bridge, sometimes as
often as six times per week. Unfortunately, the increased traffic was not sustained.
Within a few years, service west of Penticton was again three times per week.

The Carmi Subdivision fared even worse. The country between Midway and Pen-

◁ FIGURE 10-1 *The
discontinuation of
through freight and
passenger service in 1961
and 1964 respectively left
only way-freights
operating on the Kettle
Valley Railway. This
train of only two empty
"OCS" gondola cars
bound for Penticton is
seen in the cut at Mile
61.5 (Princeton
Subdivision) near the top
of the Jura Loops.* PHOTO
BY BARRIE SANFORD

ticton remained essentially as remote and undeveloped as when the railway was built more than half a century earlier. With little supporting traffic and many wooden trestles in Myra Canyon eventually needing renewal, CP Rail quietly stopped running trains west of Beaverdell in May 1973 and in 1978 permission was granted to remove the rails on the entire line. Track between Midway and Mile 67.9 was removed in 1979. Efforts were made to preserve the track between Penticton and Myra Canyon as a tourist railway. The scenery on the line was the equal of any tourist railway in North America, but the economic difficulties were overwhelming, and track on the remainder of the line was removed in late 1980. With the through Coast-to-Kootenay link now broken, Penticton could only be reached by rail from Spences Bridge. It was the eastern terminus of a remnant railroad.

In 1979 rails were also removed from the Osoyoos Subdivision south of the new mill at Okanagan Falls. Fruit traffic had been almost the sole traffic on the line south of that point, and with the complete loss of fruit traffic to trucking competition during the early 1970s the line had become redundant less than three decades after having been completed. In 1980 the spur from Merritt to Nicola was also deleted.

By 1980 forest products represented practically the only traffic on the former KVR. Lumber and chips moved from the various mills west to the mainline at Spences Bridge for shipment east or to the coast. Incoming loads were few. An economic downturn in 1982 significantly reduced the lumber trade, and resulted in the virtual demise of chip transportation as a source of revenue. Train service between Penticton and Merritt was reduced to twice per week, and never returned to former levels when economic conditions improved. Most of the passing tracks on the KVR became storage sidings for surplus freight cars awaiting a traffic upturn. Some of the cars sat unmoved for several years.

In April 1985 CP Rail announced that it was closing its station and servicing facilities at Penticton. Only seven people remained on staff at the time, and six of these were reassigned to Merritt, where the few diesel locomotives allocated to the line were thereafter also based. In April 1986 almost all trackage was removed from Penticton yard. On September 17, 1986 the roundhouse in Penticton was demolished, leaving only a few sheds and a rundown station as reminders of what was once the busy headquarters of an vibrant railway.

Through the remaining years of the 1980s freight traffic on the remnants of the KVR continued to decline. Only five customers of consequence remained on the railway, a miniscule traffic base for the 190 miles of railway from Spences Bridge eastward across the mountains to Penticton and south to Okanagan Falls. Some people, including shippers, accused CP Rail of deliberately discouraging traffic in an effort to speed its exit from the railway business in the region. Perhaps it was true, In any case, increasing amounts of lumber left the mills by truck.

FIGURE 10-2

PRINCETON SUBDIVISION			
Miles from Penticton	STATIONS	Train Order Office Signals	Car Capacity Sidings
.0	PENTICTON ....ΣΥΚ	N3	Yard
	9.5		
9.5	WEST SUMMERLAND	W3	19
	6.0		
15.5	FAULDER		65
	16.9		
32.4	THIRSK		28
	13.3		
45.7	JELLICOE		29
	14.4		
60.1	JURA		27
	10.4		
70.5	PRINCETON ....ΣΥ	OD	38
	11.8		
82.3	COALMONT		27
	4.0		
86.3	TULAMEEN		36
	6.7		
93.0	MANNING		65
	15.7		
108.7	BROOKMERE ....W		64
	11.5		
120.2	KINGSVALE		19
	17.9		
138.1	MERRITT ....ΣΥΚ	MR	57
	4.8		
142.9	COYLE		7
	14.7		
157.6	DOT		25
	20.2		
177.8	SPENCES BRIDGE ....ΣΥΚ	RN	Yard
	Jct. Thompson Sub.		
	Rules 41 and 44 apply. Rule 93A applies.		

FIGURE 10-2 *In 1961, all trackage west of Penticton was consolidated into the Princeton Subdivision. The 177.8 miles made it the longest subdivision on the Canadian Pacific system. After abandonment of the Carmi and Osoyoos Subdivisions during the 1970s it became the only subdivision on the former Kettle Valley Railway.* COLLECTION OF BARRIE SANFORD

△ FIGURE 10-3 *This eastbound way-freight climbing Brodie Loop just west of Brookmere barely disturbs the immense solitude of the Coldwater Valley. The view is looking southwest towards Coquihalla Pass, with July Mountain in the distance. The Coquihalla Highway now cuts across the hillside on the right.* PHOTO BY BARRIE SANFORD

◁ FIGURE 10-4 *No longer needed in a new railroad age, the water tower and section house at Chute Lake sit in the summer sun in this photo taken in 1970.* PHOTO BY BARRIE SANFORD

In 1988 CP Rail committed itself to construction of what it termed a Lumber Reload Centre at Campbell Creek near Kamloops. The plan was to have mills ship their lumber by truck to the reload centre, where forklifts would "reload" the lumber onto bulkhead flatcars for transportation to the main markets in the Midwest American states. By so doing it would no longer be necessary to provide rail service directly to the mills. The Kettle Valley Railway was approaching its final days.

FIGURES 10-5 & 10-6 *The loss of through freight traffic had the most dramatic impact on the remote Carmi Subdivision, where the only freight customer was the Highland Bell mine at Beaverdell. Train service on the Carmi Subdivision withered, finally being discontinued between Penticton and Beaverdell in 1973.*

FIGURE 10-5 shows Extra 8608 East at Lakevale where it has stopped to add several work cars to the string of empty boxcars being moved to Midway. FIGURE 10-6 shows Extra 8686 East passing Arawana with Okanagan Lake as a backdrop. The fishplates between the rails of the passing track and the siding show that the rails had been disconnected and the passing track removed from service. Passing tracks had become unnecessary on a rail line with only three trains per week each way.

FIGURE 10-7

△ FIGURE 10-7 *The Fairbanks-Morse diesel locomotives produced by the Canadian Locomotive Company for the CPR in the early 1950s were loved fondly by many railfans. Most such units spent the majority of their working lives on the Kootenay and Kettle Valley Divisions, where opportunities for superlative action photographs abounded. This picture shows a lone "F-M" crossing West Fork Canyon Creek bridge with a short train for Midway.* PHOTO BY BARRIE SANFORD

FIGURE 10-8

△ FIGURE 10-8 *"F-M" 4081 eastbound with a freight of empty boxcars crosses the 100-foot-long pony truss bridge over the Kettle River at Mile 26.9 (Carmi Subdivision) near Rhone. Engineman Cliff Inkster watches the camera as the train passes. This bridge was installed during a 12-hour period on April 29, 1929 and replaced a wooden bridge built during the line's original construction. After the railway's abandonment it was moved four miles downstream where it now serves as a roadway bridge.* PHOTO BY BARRIE SANFORD

▷ FIGURE 10-10 *A westbound freight train exits from the 162-foot-long "Little Tunnel" at Mile 122.0 (Carmi Subdivision) on the descent from Chute Lake to Penticton.*
PHOTO BY BARRIE SANFORD

▽ FIGURE 10-9 *An important part of Okanagan rail operations was the barge service on Okanagan Lake, which was used primarily to move Okanagan fruit traffic north to the CPR mainline for transport to Calgary and other major prairie markets. Here, switcher 7111 loads cars onto a barge at Penticton on a windy summer evening.* PHOTO BY BARRIE SANFORD

FIGURE 10-9

FIGURE 10-10

FIGURES 10-11 & 10-12 *Remnants of the steam age survived longer on the KVR than on the mainline, where most such structures were demolished in the mid-1960s. The Kingsvale water tower was demolished in 1974. The four-stall roundhouse at Brookmere, built in 1949 to replace the earlier three-stall roundhouse, was sold to a local resident in 1969 for $525 and was disassembled for salvage the following year.*

☐ FIGURES 10-13 & 10-14 *The final train to operate over the tracks in Myra Canyon was among the most interesting. Between June 20 and 23, 1973 the Canadian Broadcasting Corporation filmed segments of its major television series "The National Dream" using former CPR locomotive 136 in spectacular Myra Canyon on the Carmi Subdivision. FIGURE 10-13 shows 136 — temporarily renumbered 148 for this shooting sequence — and two cars eastbound on the 429-foot-long frame trestle at Mile 88.2. FIGURE 10-14 shows diesel 8509 helping 136 over the same trestle, viewed from across West Fork Canyon Creek.*

FIGURE 10-15 PHOTO BY LANCE CAMP

FIGURES 10-15 & 10-16 *During 1977 the Provincial Museum train, using former CPR steam engine 3716, made a tour over the Kettle Valley Railway from Spences Bridge through to Penticton and Osoyoos. Lance Camp captured this pair of fine pictures of steam back on the Kettle Valley Railway after an absence of nearly a quarter century. FIGURE 10-15 shows the train at Osoyoos. FIGURE 10-16 shows the train crossing Trout Creek Bridge on its return run to Spences Bridge. The 3716's trip to Osoyoos was the last train to operate south of Okanagan Falls.*

FIGURE 10-16 PHOTO BY LANCE CAMP

FIGURE 10-17

FIGURE 10-18

 FIGURE 10-17
Fruit traffic was the lifeblood of the Osoyoos Subdivision, and when truck competition captured the fruit trade traffic on the line south of Penticton withered. Here, "F-M" 8604 skirts along the shore of Skaha Lake on its way to Osoyoos with an empty gondola car and three empty fruit reefers. The engine will spend the day in Osoyoos, then return with the loaded cars for the evening barge to Kelowna. PHOTO BY BARRIE SANFORD

FIGURE 10-18
Both Oliver and Osoyoos had stations, even though no formal passenger train service ever operated on the Osoyoos Subdivision. The stations were built to administer the substantial freight traffic business with the fruit packing houses and a small number of sawmills along the line. The local agent would arrange for freight cars to be provided and would handle waybills and other freight matters. The station at Oliver is shown here.
PHOTO BY BARRIE SANFORD

FIGURE 10-20

△ FIGURE 10-20 *Passenger train service on the Kettle Valley Railway returned briefly on the Victoria Day weekend in 1983 and again in 1984 when the British Columbia Chapter of the National Railway Historical Society sponsored its "Okanagan Express" tour from Vancouver to Penticton and return. Here passengers enjoy a photo stop at Brookmere beside the double-spouted water tower.* PHOTO BY BARRIE SANFORD

◁ FIGURE 10-19 *In 1976 CP Rail introduced new motive power to the KVR in the form of GP-38 diesels, which were light enough to allow operation on the 85-pound rail which predominated on the rail line. Several units were assigned to Penticton, with usually one more at Merritt. Here, a pair of new GP-38's pilots 20 loads of lumber down the Nicola Valley a mile west of Dot.* PHOTO BY BARRIE SANFORD

▽ FIGURES 10-21 & 10-22 *Two stations: Midway and West Summerland. The highly attractive station at Midway has fortunately been relocated and preserved as a museum. The West Summerland station was less fortunate, and has been demolished.*

FIGURE 10-21 PHOTO BY BARRIE SANFORD

FIGURE 10-22 PHOTO BY BARRIE SANFORD

▷ FIGURE 10-23 *In 1984 Coquihalla Pass again became the scene of great construction activity as work started on the spectacular — and controversial — Coquihalla Highway. This interesting photograph taken in June 1985 from the south side of Coquihalla Canyon shows the steel arch span on the new highway across Dry Gulch as a cross brace is positioned by an overhead cable trolley in preparation for the highway's official opening on May 16, 1986. At the bottom of the photo are the remains of the 405-foot-long wooden frame trestle on the Kettle Valley Railway at Mile 20.7 (Coquihalla Subdivision), which was blown up on September 28, 1969 in a demolition exercise by the troops of the Canadian Forces.*

Interestingly, the steel for the new bridge represented one of the last destination loads transported on the KVR. The steel was delivered by rail to Brodie and transferred to trucks for hauling the last 16 miles to the bridge site. There was no siding at Brodie at that time so trains merely waited on the main track — sometimes several hours — while the steel was unloaded. Such a luxury was permissable on the KVR in 1985, as only one train at a time was being operated. PHOTO BY BARRIE SANFORD

Kettle Valley Railway Dateline

1965 - 1988

1966-08-01	Princeton Subdivision crew layover point changed from Brookmere to Merritt and Brookmere station closed.
1967-02-09	Canadian Centennial "Confederation Train" ran from Spences Bridge to Midway.
1969-09-28	Canadian Forces personnel blew up 405-foot-long frame trestle at Mile 20.7 (Coquihalla Subdivision) in demolition exercise.
1972-05-31	Last day of operation of CPR barge service on Okanagan Lake.
1973-05-19	Engine 8724 ran from Penticton to Midway and return with last regular run on the Carmi Subdivision west of Beaverdell. No other trains ran over this section of track until 1973-06-12.
1973-06-12	Engine 8509 ran from Nelson to Penticton with steam locomotive 136 in tow in preparation for filming of "The National Dream" in Myra Canyon. Rods were put on 136 at Penticton June 17 and 18.
1973-06-19	Engine 8509 ran from Penticton to Myra Canyon with steam locomotive 136 for filming June 20 to 23. Train returned to Penticton June 23 and rods removed from 136 June 24.
1973-06-25	Engine 8509 ran from Penticton to Nelson with steam locomotive 136 following filming. This was the final train over the section of track between Penticton and Beaverdell. Occasional freight service continued between Midway and Beaverdell to serve the Highland Bell mine.
1974-11-08	Canadian Transport Commission approved closure of West Summerland, Princeton and Merritt stations.
1977-04-05	Four carloads of salt delivered to Rock Creek from Midway. This was reported to be the final load west of Midway.
1977-07-05	Provincial Museum train on display at Penticton. The next day it ran from Penticton to Oliver, and the day after from Oliver to Osoyoos. This was last train south of Okanagan Falls.
1978-06-21	Canadian Transport Commission approved abandonment of the Osoyoos Subdivision between Osoyoos and Okanagan Falls.
1978-08-13	Provincial Museum Train arrived at Midway from Grand Forks.
1978-12-22	Canadian Transport Commission approved abandonment of the Carmi Subdivision.
1981-04-30	Canadian Forces personnel blew up the steel arch truss bridge across Slide Creek at Mile 25.8 (Coquihalla Subdivision) in demolition exercise.
1983-05-21	Engines 8836 and 8839 operated "Okanagan Express" passenger excursion train from Vancouver to Penticton over KVR. The following day train operated Penticton-Princeton return and Penticton-Jellicoe return. On the third day it returned to Vancouver.
1984-05-19	Engines 8838 and 8839 operated "Okanagan Express" passenger excursion train from Vancouver to Penticton over KVR. The following day train operated Penticton-Jellicoe return. On the third day it returned to Vancouver.
1985-04-25	CP Rail announced that it would close its roundhouse and station in Penticton.
1986-02-14	Former Brookmere station destroyed by fire.
1986-09-17	Penticton roundhouse demolished.
1987-07-18	Coquihalla Canyon Recreation Area at Quintette Tunnels at Othello officially opened.
1987-07-20	Brookmere water tower relocated for preservation.
1988-06-04	Andrew McCulloch memorial at Midway officially dedicated.

FIGURE 10-23

FIGURE 10-24 PHOTO BY BARRIE SANFORD

☐ FIGURES 10-24 & 10-25 *Two GP-38's lift a short train of empty bulkhead lumber flats up the Jura Hill. FIGURE 10-24 was taken from Mile 63.5 on the middle loop, looking down at the train at Mile 65.0 just east of the former passing track at Belfort. FIGURE 10-25 shows the train passing Separation Lake at the top of the upper loop. Careful inspection will reveal the remains of a rail spur down to the lake.*

▷ FIGURE 10-26 *A lengthy train was in order this day as engines 3001 and 3003 follow the east shore of Otter Lake bound for Princeton and Penticton. Such trains were rare. By the mid-1980s trains did not generally exceed twenty cars.* PHOTO BY BARRIE SANFORD

FIGURE 10-25 PHOTO BY BARRIE SANFORD

FIGURE 10-26

▷ FIGURE 10-28 *Despite the many inroads of civilization in other parts of the province, much of the area traversed by the Kettle Valley Railway system remained little changed from the days of the railway's construction more than three-quarters of a century ago. This picture of a train climbing up the valley of Spearing Creek just east of Brookmere is one of the author's favourites.* PHOTO BY BARRIE SANFORD

▽ FIGURE 10-27 *In 1987 the Quintette Tunnels at Othello were formally designated the Coquihalla Canyon Recreation Area. Though one of the smallest parks in the province it is one of the most impressive, the steep rock faces and thundering river gorge offering an awesome spectacle of nature's grandeur and a reminder of the difficult conditions under which the early railway surveyors and labourers worked. A great deal of credit is due the citizens of Hope for championing the cause of park designation for the tunnels. The freshly fallen rock on the former rail roadbed is evidence that the Coquihalla has yet to forgive its intruders.* PHOTO BY BARRIE SANFORD

FIGURE 10-27

FIGURE 10-28

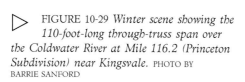 FIGURE 10-29 *Winter scene showing the 110-foot-long through-truss span over the Coldwater River at Mile 116.2 (Princeton Subdivision) near Kingsvale.* PHOTO BY BARRIE SANFORD

CHAPTER 11

The Final Days

The Kettle Valley Railway: 1989-1990

IN EARLY 1989 AN ARTICLE IN AN OKANAGAN NEWSPAPER STATED THAT CP RAIL WAS IN THE ''FINAL STAGES'' OF negotiations with Weyerhaeuser Canada for arrangements to transport lumber by truck from the company's sawmills at Okanagan Falls and Princeton to CP Rail's new Lumber Reload Centre near Kamloops. At that time the mills were being served by two trains per week, a train eastbound from Merritt to Penticton and Okanagan Falls on Mondays and Wednesdays, with the return run the following day. The two mills represented the only shippers on the 150 miles of trackage east of Merritt. Three other mills were at Merritt. A weekday ''turn'' from Merritt to Spences Bridge and back served these customers and the rail cars delivered from the mills at Okanagan Falls and Princeton. As negotiations continued each train leaving Penticton picked up a few more stored cars from the sidings along the KVR.

No announcement of the conclusion of the negotiations was made, and on March 1, 1989 — with only a few hours advance warning — the last revenue train left Okanagan Falls and Penticton. Train service continued to the Weyerhaeuser mill at Princeton on a twice weekly basis until the end of April, then it too was withdrawn. In early May a work train traversed almost the entire line between Merritt and Okanagan Falls performing shutdown preparation and salvaging surplus track material. On May 12, 1989 engine 8245 gathered up all remaining cars in the Merritt yard and gave long, symbolic blasts on the diesel air horn as it pulled away from the Nicola Valley community and headed for Spences Bridge. It was the last train to do so. No other trains were to run on the tracks of the Kettle Valley Railway.[11]

Throughout the remainder of 1989 and into early 1990 there was much discussion about the silent tracks of the Kettle Valley Railway. Proposals were presented to reactivate the railway for tourist train operations or for filming movies. Suggestions were made to convert the right-of-way into a hiking or bicycle trail. An American company even put forth the ambitious proposal to construct a coal-fired thermal power plant at Princeton and upgrade the rail line between Spences Bridge and Princeton for delivery of thermal coal from the East Kootenays. In the meantime the tracks became overgrown with weeds and blocked by rockfalls. In places nearby landowners erected fences across the tracks in anticipation that they would fall heir to the discarded right-of-way.

However, a year after the last CP Rail train had run over the line it became clear that no reactivation of the line was to be forthcoming. In June 1990 the National Transportation Agency authorized abandonment of the rail line. As of July 21, 1990 ''The KV'' had passed into history.

◁ FIGURE 11-1
The black clouds gathering over Princeton seem symbolic of the darkening times for the former Kettle Valley Railway as GP-38 units 3001 and 3003 descend Jura Hill at Mile 62 (Princeton Subdivision) with a train from Penticton. But the short train length is more telling that train operation on ''The KV'' is nearly finished.
PHOTO BY BARRIE SANFORD

△ FIGURE 11-2 *Engines 5024 and 5022 are pushing a snowplow as they speed up the middle loop of Jura Hill headed for Penticton on March 7, 1989. The two engines are not clearing the line for revenue trains. The last revenue train had left Penticton six days earlier, and 5024 and 5022 are going to Penticton only to pick up empty cars and cars of salvage material which they will return to Merritt the following day. This was the final plow train over "The KV" and the second to last train to Penticton.* PHOTO BY J. GLENN ROEMER

▷ FIGURE 11-3 *In another winter scene early in 1989 engines 3056 and 3073 pilot three revenue cars westbound across the 103-foot-long through-plate girder span over the Coldwater River at Mile 112.9 (Princeton Subdivision) at Brodie. Behind the train is the 108-foot-long deck truss bridge at Mile 4.1 of the abandoned Coquihalla Subdivision.* PHOTO BY LANCE CAMP

FIGURES 11-4 & 11-5 *The date is April 25, 1989 and in FIGURE 11-5 engines 8213 and 8219 have just exited from Parr Tunnel at Mile 75.8 Princeton Subdivision with their train of two loaded side dump cars and two cabooses bound for Princeton. The cars of ballast are to be spread on the track closer to Princeton. The extra caboose is to accommodate local residents and railfans making a "last ride" over the railway, an unofficial but appreciated supplement to all trains during the final few weeks of operation which no doubt occurred without endorsement from Windsor Station.*

In FIGURE 11-4 the engines are seen later on the same day as they cross Thalia trestle at Mile 102.7 Princeton Subdivision on the return run to Merritt. The engines have brought back eight empty lumber flatcars. The empty lumber cars were no longer required; the last lumber to leave the Princeton mill by rail had gone the previous week. PHOTO BY LANCE CAMP

FIGURE 11-5 PHOTO BY J. GLENN RC

Kettle Valley Railway Dateline

1989 - 1990

1989-03-01 Engines 5024 and 5022 ran from Okanagan Falls to Merritt with the last revenue train east of Princeton.

1989-03-07 Engines 5024 and 5022 ran with plow train from Merritt to Penticton.

1989-03-08 Engines 5022 and 5024 ran from Penticton to Merritt after picking up salvagable material from Penticton yard.

1989-03-09 Engines 5024 and 5022 ran from Merritt to Jura and return to pick up one gondola car left on Jura siding. No further trains operated east of Princeton until 1989-05-08.

1989-04-27 Engines 8213 and 8219 ran from Merritt to Princeton and return to pick up seven empty bulkhead flats from Princeton mill. This was the last regular train east of Brookmere. No further trains operated over line east of Brookmere until 1989-05-08.

1989-05-02 Engines 8213 and 8219 ran from Merritt to Brookmere and return to transport Caboose 437216 to Brookmere for permanent display.

1989-05-04 Engines 8219 and 8213 ran work train from Spences Bridge to Brodie then back to Merritt. Train was filling bridge water barrels and salvaging material.

1989-05-08 Engines 8219 and 8213 ran work train from Merritt to Penticton continuing salvage work.

1989-05-09 Engines 8219 and 8213 ran light from Penticton to north end of Okanagan Falls trestle and return, then through to Merritt with work train. This was the last train over the line east of Merritt.

1989-05-12 Engine 8245 ran from Merritt to Spences Bridge with seven loads and 28 empties, comprising 1917 tons. This was the last train to run over the former Kettle Valley Railway.

1990-06-21 National Transportation Agency authorized CP Rail to abandon Princeton Subdivision effective 1990-07-21.

FIGURE 11-6

FIGURE 11-6

FIGURE 11-7

FIGURE 11-6 On *April 27, 1989 engines 8213 and 8219 ran from Merritt to Princeton to remove seven unloaded bulkhead lumber flats from the Princeton mill for return to Merritt. This trip marked the end of train service east of Merritt with the exception of a few work train movements in the following two weeks. Here the westbound train passes through Brookmere, the former divisional point at the divide between the Fraser River and Columbia River systems.* PHOTO BY BARRIE SANFORD

FIGURE 11-7 *Manual Block System Clearance authorizing Work Extra 8245 to make the final run from Merritt to Spences Bridge.* COLLECTION OF J. GLENN ROEMER

FIGURE 11-8 *One of the more unusual train movements during the final days of operation was on May 2, 1989, when caboose 437216 was moved from Merritt to Brookmere. The wooden caboose had been on display at Merritt for several years previously, but was donated by the City of Merritt to the citizens of Brookmere and moved by CP Rail free of charge as a modest tribute to Brookmere's railroad heritage. Here we see the train at Kingsvale.* PHOTO BY BARRIE SANFORD

FIGURE 11-9

△ FIGURE 11-9 *Engines 8219 and 8213 are seen in this photo piloting an eastbound work train across the pile trestle over the south end of Otter Lake at Mile 86.6 (Princeton Subdivision) on May 8, 1989. Regular service had now ceased and the train was engaged in filling bridge water barrels and salvaging material. This was the final train eastbound from Merritt.* PHOTO BY DAVE WILKIE

FIGURE 11-10

▷ FIGURE 11-10
May 9, 1989 was the date of the final train westward from Penticton through to Merritt. As the train crew boarded locomotives 8213 and 8219 in Penticton that morning they decided to take an unauthorized run down the Okanagan Falls spur as a final view of the line before their departure westward. This picture shows the two locomotives, without caboose, trundling along the shore of Skaha Lake for the final time. PHOTO BY DAVE WILKIE

FIGURE 11-11

△ FIGURE 11-11 *The massive steel bridge across Trout Creek just west of Penticton symbolized the railway admiringly dubbed ''McCulloch's Wonder.'' But it would carry no more trains after this train — Work Extra 8219 West — passed over it on May 9, 1989 with the final train to leave Penticton.* PHOTO BY DAVE WILKIE

▷ FIGURE 11-12 *Three days later — May 12, 1989 — train service over the tracks of the former Kettle Valley Railway ceased. Here engine 8245 arrives at Spences Bridge with the last train from Merritt. Symbolically, the train is on the final few hundred feet of the Princeton Subdivision just before its junction with the CP Rail mainline at Spences Bridge.* PHOTO BY DAVE WILKIE

FIGURE 11-12

pilogue

TRAINS NO LONGER RUN ON THE KETTLE VALLEY RAIL-
WAY. TO SOME PEOPLE THE DEMISE WAS ALL TOO PRE-
dictable. The KVR had been built in an age when all freight and
passenger movement was by rail, and the relatively light trains
of that era could tolerate the steep grades encountered in crossing the mountains of
southern British Columbia. However, when the highways and airplanes of a more
modern age stripped the KVR of its passenger, mail and high revenue freight traffic,
the railway's steep grades took on new significance. The remaining bulk commodities
traffic required longer and heavier trains to remain remunerative at the low tariffs
which these commodities commanded. In that respect the Kettle Valley Railway fell
victim to evolution.

One Canadian Pacific official was even more blunt in his assessment: ''Of all
the blunders in railway building history the CPR's southern British Columbia rail line
is the greatest.''[12] Certainly the KVR's financial ledgers would have supported this
viewpoint.

But the financial ledgers do not tell the entire story. The Kettle Valley Railway
halted the flow of Kootenay trade going to the United States at a critical time in British Columbia's history. The railway also spurred the development of the province, including the highways and airports which later relegated the railway into obscurity.
In that regard the KVR's value cannot be discounted merely because it is no longer
in operation.

And as one drives over the new Coquihalla Highway, built by massive taxpayer-
funded cost overruns, one can easily wonder if the Kettle Valley Railway would not
still be running were the governments not so willing to finance road and airport construction far in excess of the revenue collected from fuel taxes and user fees. The highways too cannot approach the KVR's unblemished safety record. Deaths by highway
accident now seem so common as to be without news value or concern. Perhaps that
fact alone is more tragic than the loss of any railway.

Evolution may have destroyed the Kettle Valley Railway, but evolution cannot
wipe out the fact that for an entire generation the KVR was the lifeline of southern
British Columbia. Nor can it wipe out the fact that the Kettle Valley Railway, though
it never made a penny profit for the CPR which built it, paid the people of British
Columbia handsomely in the development of their province. Whatever else may be
said, the rails of ''The KV'' were not laid in error.

◁ FIGURE 12-1
*Twilight on the
Kettle Valley Railway at
Brookmere.* PHOTO BY
BARRIE SANFORD

ACKNOWLEDGEMENTS

A pictorial book covering the time span of more than a century is naturally the work of many people. Unfortunately, the identity of the photographer of many of the images used in this book is not known, so it has not been possible for me to identify each photograph with its creator, as I would liked to have done. For those photographers whose works are not directly acknowledged in the photo credits I would like to extend my recognition and appreciation.

Nicholas Morant of Canadian Pacific and Lumb Stock of Penticton took many of the photographs in this book. More recent contributions come from Lance Camp, Norm Gidney, Gib Kennedy, Andre Morin, Bill Presley, Glenn Roemer, Joe Smuin and Dave Wilkie. I would also like to extend thanks to Randy Manuel and Dianne Truant of the Penticton Museum, to Jim Shields of Canadian Pacific and to Vintage Visuals of Calgary for their assistance.

A special note of appreciation is extended to those rail photographers who took so many fine photos of the final days of KVR operations in April and May 1989. Only a very small number of the photographs sent to me could be used in this book, but it is gratifying that the historic moment was so well documented.

Barrie Sanford
1990

NOTES

1. James Douglas, *British Columbia Historical Quarterly*, Vol. 2 (Victoria, 1938), p. 81.

2. Walter Vaughan, *The Life and Works of Sir William Van Horne* (New York: Century Co., 1920), p. 229.

3. Victoria *Colonist* (1901-07-16), p. 8.

4. Vancouver *Province* (1902-04-11), p. 1.

5. Vancouver *Province* (1905-09-18), p. 1.

6. Vancouver *Province* (1912-03-04), p. 1.

7. Victoria *Colonist* (1916-09-17), p. 1.

8. The Quintette Tunnels were numbered Tunnels 10, 11, 12 and 13 although in fact there were only 12 tunnels on the Coquihalla Subdivision. Tunnel 9 was planned at the time the Quintette Tunnels had been started but was never built.

9. *Penticton Herald* (1939-02-02), p. 1.

10 *Canadian Railway & Marine World*, January 1924.

11. Curiously, a tiny piece of KVR track remained in service after May 1989, that being the connecting link between CP Rail and the Burlington Northern at Grand Forks, which was part of the original line to Republic started in 1901.

12. J.G. Sullivan, former CPR chief engineer, in a private letter to Andrew McCulloch 1937-03-02.

INDEX

Allison Pass 9

Board of Transport Commissioners
  108-10, 122
Boundary District 8, 9, 10, 15, 33,
  76, 122, 129
Brookmere 34, 35, 36, 61, 76, 94,
  107, 129
Budd Cars 108

CP Rail 129, 130, 151
Canadian Pacific Railway:
  Mainline 5, 6, 8, 25, 75, 77, 107,
  110, 122
  For other references to Canadian
  Pacific see specific item desired.
Carmi Subdividion 129
Coast-to-Kootenay railway 6, 8, 9,
  20, 34, 36, 61, 62, 110, 130
Columbia & Kootenay Railway 6,
  7, 8, 15
Columbia & Western Railway
  8, 15
Copper Mountain Line/Subdivision
  77, 93, 94
Coquihalla (station) 76
Coquihalla Agreement 36, 61-62, 94
Coquihalla Line/Subdivision
  61, 62, 75, 77, 93, 94, 95, 107,
  121, 161
Coquihalla Pass 9, 25, 34, 36, 61,
  62, 75, 77, 93, 107, 121, 161
Corbin Daniel 6, 8
Coryell, J.A. 7, 8
Crowsnest Pass rail line 8, 33

Dewdney, Edgar 6, 9, 33
Diamond Vale Collieries 28
Douglas Lake Cattle Company 28
Dunsmuir, James 8, 25

Esquimalt & Nanaimo Railway 9

Grand Forks 15, 18, 33
Grand Forks union station 18
Great Northern Railway:
  Boundary District Line 15, 16
  Canadian Pacific Railway 7, 33,
  36, 94
  Coquihalla Pass line 33, 36, 61,
  62, 94
  Crowsnest Pass line 8, 33

Mainline 7, 33
  Republic line 16
  Sandon line 7
  Similkameen Valley line 33,94
  Tulameen Valley line 36, 94, 107

Hill, James 7, 8, 15, 16, 33, 34, 61,
  62
Hill, Louis 62
Holland, Tracy 15
Hope 5, 7, 9, 25, 34, 36, 61, 75, 76
Hope Mountains 9, 10, 20, 28, 33,
  34, 36, 61
Hot Air Line 16

Inland Coke & Coal Co. 28

Kettle River/Valley 8, 15, 33
Kettle River Valley Railway 15, 18,
  34
Kettle Valley Division 77, 93, 107,
  108, 122
Kettle Valley Express 75
Kettle Valley Lines 17
Kettle Valley Railway:
  Canadian Pacific Railway 34, 61,
  75, 77, 93
  Chartered 16
  Conceived 5, 15
  Construction 34, 35
  Completed 36
  Freight service 76, 107, 110, 121,
  129, 130, 151, 161
  Locomotives 75-76, 93, 107-8, 130
  Passenger service 36, 75, 107, 108,
  110, 121, 122
  Renamed 18
  Route chosen 34
  For other references to KVR see
  specific item desired.
Kootenay District: 5, 9, 15, 33, 62,
  75, 129
Kootenay Express 75

Mackenzie, Alexander 5, 121
McCulloch, Andrew 34, 62, 75
McCulloch (station) 34
McCulloch's Wonder 34
Merritt 26, 28, 34, 35, 36, 76, 77,
  129, 130, 151
Merritt Line/Subdivision 75, 77,
  108, 122

Midway 8, 15, 34, 36, 75, 129, 130
Myra Canyon 93, 130

National Transportation Agency 151
Nelson & Fort Sheppard Railway 6
Nicola 26
Nicola Branch 25, 28, 36, 77
Nicola, Kamloops & Similkameen
  Railway 25, 26
Nicola Pine Mills 76
Nicola Valley Coal & Coke Co. 26
Nicola Valley Lumber Company 28
Nicola Valley Railway 25
North Fork Line/Subdivision 17, 20, 94
Northern Pacific Railroad 6, 7

Okanagan Falls 77, 93, 129, 130, 151
Okanagan lake 34, 35, 129
Oliver 77, 95
Osoyoos 77, 95
Osoyoos Line/Subdivision 77, 93,
  95, 130

Penticton 34, 35, 36, 62, 76, 77,
  93, 108, 121, 129, 130, 151
Princeton 9, 33, 36, 76, 77, 94,
  107, 129, 151
Princeton Line/Subdivision 93

Republic & Kettle River Railway 15

Shaughnessy, Thomas 8, 26, 28, 33,
  61, 62
Similkameen River/Valley 9, 26, 33
Skaha Lake 77, 93
South Penticton 35
Spences Bridge 9, 25, 26, 75, 77,
  122, 130, 151
Spokane & British Columbia Railway
  15, 20
Spokane Falls & Northern Railway 6

Tulameen Agreement 36, 94

Van Horne, William 7, 8
Vancouver, Victoria & Eastern Railway
  8, 16, 36, 61

Warren, James 34, 62
Washington & Great Northern
  Railway 16
Windermere Subdivision 122

Train 12 at Chute Lake, 1950 PHOTO BY GIB KENNEDY

About the Author

Barrie Sanford is no stranger to the Kettle Valley Railway. His book *McCulloch's Wonder*, published in 1977, has gone through four printings and continues to be one of the bestselling books dealing with the history of a Canadian railway. Indeed, it was at the suggestion of many readers of *McCulloch's Wonder* that Barrie was prompted to produce his latest work, *Steel Rails and Iron Men*.

Barrie has written widely on other railway and technical subjects. His book *The Pictorial History of Railroading in British Columbia* was one of ten finalists selected for the prestigious Eaton's Book Award in 1981. He has also written for *Trains* and other national or international magazines.

Barrie holds a Civil Engineering degree from the University of British Columbia and a Master of Business Administration degree from Simon Fraser University. His career path has been in passenger transportation where he has been involved with the management of urban and rural bus systems and transportation for the handicapped.